A Leather Dog Collar

Charles Stelland with all good wishes

A Leather
Dog Collar

Charles Stallard

dinas

© Charles Stallard & Y Lolfa Cyf., 2004
First impression: 2004

This contents of this book are subject to copyright and may not be reproduced by any means without the prior written consent of the publishers.

Cover photograph reproduced by kind permission
of Newsquest Midlands South Ltd.

ISBN: 0 86243 740 7

Dinas is an imprint of Y Lolfa

Printed and published in Wales
by Y Lolfa Cyf., Talybont, Ceredigion SY24 5AP
e-mail ylolfa@ylolfa.com
website www.ylolfa.com
tel. (01970) 832 304
fax 832 782

Contents

Contents

Acknowledgements

First, I should like to thank Daphne for all her love and support to me as well as to Dennis and Jubilee.

Thanks are also due to the people of the parishes of Droitwich Spa and St. Mark's, Pensnett for their support, while I was in the Midlands. Since I moved to Aberystwyth, Jubilee, Daphne and I have made many very kind friends here, too.

The illustrations help to enliven this book; therefore, I should like to express my appreciation to the illustrators, Jean McCambridge and Lesley Hopkins.

Finally, thanks to Moira Smith for her editorial help.

Introduction

THESE STORIES ORIGINATE From time spent in the Midlands, mainly in the parishes of Droitwich Spa and Pensnett, but end up in Aberystwyth, to where my wife, Daphne, and I have retired. During this period, we saw our children, Andrew, Mary and John, grow up. Two of them are married and we now have four grandchildren, but here you will meet them through the eyes of our dachshund dogs, Dennis and Jubilee.

Like all dog-owners, we soon found that Dennis and Jubilee not only saw themselves as part of the family but expected to be included in all our activities, even down to writing a monthly newsletter for the parish magazine. These newsletters form the basis for the stories.

Dennis we named after Dennis the Dachshund from the radio Children's Hour favourite, 'Toy Town'. He has some of that dog's characteristics; he is manipulative, quick to seize the main chance, and not a little devious.

Jubilee arrived to celebrate twenty-five years of my ministry in the Church of England. He has his own ways of influencing events; he is not as direct as Dennis was but is just as effective.

Lost in the Fog!

FOG UP THE CANAL. Fog down the canal. Fog seeping up the Holloway. Fog swirling across St. Peter's Fields, and even finding its way up the steps of the pulpit. Fog in the Rectory study.

In case you're wondering what the dickens this is about, I must admit that, usually, the Rectory is no bleak house. That is, when they remember to put the gas fire on and I can stretch myself out in front of it, with no one to disturb me. These November mornings have been quite a trial. We began with fog. Then, there's been rain, cold winds, and sometimes a dreary mixture of all three. Every morning, however, from Monday to Friday, I go for a walk along the canal, across the fields, or up and down the Worcester Road. However, when it comes to Saturdays, I draw the line by pulling on the lead.

'Who's going to take Dennis for a walk?'

The family are not enthusiastic. I close my eyes tighter and try to sink down further into my blankets. If I were a chameleon, I'd turn blue. One particularly nasty Saturday morning, I got my own back.

The rain was pouring down. The Rector put me on my collar and lead, and dragged me to the front door. It was terrible. Undeterred, I was pulled over the doorstep and out on to the pavement. The Rector started walking down the road, his umbrella in one hand and my lead in the other. A car passed by and hooted. The driver waved. The Rector waved back and went on walking.

A couple of people on foot gave the Rector an odd look. Somewhat puzzled, he looked down, to give me an encouraging pat. I wasn't there – the collar was empty. I had managed to slip my head out and was sitting under the porch, waiting for the door to open. I'm not daft – but clearly, the passers-by had some doubts about the Rector. The invisible dachshund strikes again.

Christmas will soon be here. Presents, wrapping paper and string are lying around on tables, usually out of my reach.

A visitor asked brightly, 'And what is Dennis having for Christmas?'

I looked up with interest.

'A box of gift-wrapped Bonios,' came the reply.

'And what is Dennis going to give you for Christmas?'

I gave the dog's equivalent of a hard stare. Did they not know? Had they not realised, that every day of every year, I faithfully give them all that I have to give. I give them myself – Dennis.

Christmas Compensations

ON CHRISTMAS EVE, I had a stocking, or, to be more precise, an old red sock, pinned up on the cupboard next to my basket. I was told it was for Father Christmas. We had a number of visitors, but none of them turned out to be Father Christmas, for, on Christmas Day, the sock was still empty. Christmas seems to make the family forgetful, and I wasn't fooled by the excuse that Father Christmas didn't leave anything in it because I would have chewed it up in one go. The Rector's daughter says, it was most unfair of the Angels to sing, 'Good will towards men' – they should have added women. What I say is, 'What about the dogs?' To be fair to the family, I confess that I wasn't entirely left out; I did get one present – a dog sausage done up like a Christmas cracker, which I was allowed to eat in instalments. Even that wasn't from the family but from Eleanor, who is the verger at St. Peter's, but she also helps us at the Rectory.

Christmas is an odd time for dogs. By the end of it, I am told, many of us are simply thrown out on to the streets. So much for the good will. However, even in quite respectable households, routine goes by the board.

Breakfast starts at any time and seems to last all morning. Members of the family and guests, in various forms of attire, appear in the kitchen. I am totally ignored until someone says, 'Who's going to walk Dennis?'

There is a distinct lack of enthusiasm. Hedgehog-like, I curl up in my basket, pretending not to hear. With the very odd hours we keep, a dog needs his rest. However, there is no escape. I am dragged and carried down to the Red Lion. Once I am there, it's really not too bad. There are some interesting smells around, and I inspect a whole line of white posts. We go back up the Worcester Road, along the hedgerow. I always stop at the Ministry of Defence, for a good sniff. The Rector says if I am caught sniffing round the Ministry of Defence much more, we shall both be arrested for spying. If that's the case, I'll start writing my memoirs and call the book 'Bore-Catcher'.

Talking of bores, when we finally get round to Christmas Day lunch, it is always worth waiting for. Crisp crackly turkey skin gets added to my tripe and All-Bran. Scraps of turkey and pork find their way into my dish, and, after lunch, I stretch out in front of the fire, gently toasting myself, and on the lookout for the odd piece of chocolate that falls to the floor, or an unguarded plate of sausage rolls on the coffee table.

Christmas has its compensations.

Where There's a Crowd, There are Biscuits

YOU CAN'T TEACH old dogs new tricks, but young pups can learn from those of us who are mature. We had just visited the Play Group at St. Peter's Church when the Rector suggested to Kathy that she might like to visit the School. Kathy was staying with us at the Rectory. She comes from the U.S.A., where her mother is a teacher. She said that she would like to see the school as the children are the same age as those whom her mother teaches. So it was that I found myself for the first time going to St. Peter's School.

I led the way in through the playground. When the children caught sight of me, they ran, laughing and shouting, towards us. Soon, I was immersed in a crowd of children, all longing to stroke me and to pat me. Why the Rector should have been so astonished I don't know. Perhaps, he's jealous that his congregation don't greet him with the same enthusiasm.

We progressed into the school, where I immediately made for the staff-room. The teachers were having coffee and biscuits. Now, experience has taught me that, where there is a crowd having these things, crumbs and even whole biscuits have been known to land on the floor. Being a tidy hound, I make sure they are not left lying around for long. However, we were there on serious business, and I wanted to get on with the teaching. While the Headmaster took Kathy round the school, I made for a classroom, followed by the Rector in hot pursuit.

'Look, it's a sausage-dog!' shouted one of the children.

Normally, I take exception to this, but you have to make allowances for the young. The Rector stood me on one of the desks, and the children looked suitably impressed. He told them that my ancestors came from Germany and that they had been bred for hunting badgers.

'These brave little dogs, with their short legs, can easily get in to the badgers' sets. Their slim bodies enable them to tunnel in and to seek out the badgers. When attacked, the badgers can be very fierce.'

Actually, I have never seen a badger, much less hunted one. However, I thought a little yap would not come amiss. The Rector hastily put me down on the floor, where I decided to liven up the lesson up by giving a demonstration of tunnelling. I ran under the desks. The children shrieked with delight. They laughed even louder when the Rector tried to get me out, and I escaped. Finally, he scooped me up and we visited some more classrooms. The lesson was repeated, but I was not allowed to repeat my demonstration. This was a pity, as I felt the children missed the best bit.

When we left, the Headmaster thanked me for coming and said I must come again some time. The Rector smiled, but was it really necessary for him to mutter something about 'not over his dead body'?

Mud, Mud, Glorious Mud

'NO DOGS.' A good start, I thought to myself as the Rector read out the notice. I had been promised a walk and to that end, the Doctor had taken us in his car to Hanbury Hall.

'The walk doesn't take us into the grounds of the house,' he said, 'we go across the park to the Church on the top of the hill.'

So it was that the seven of us, five humans and two dogs, set off to walk from Hanbury Hall to Hanbury Church.

'Will it take long?' asked the other lady. 'I want to be back in an hour.'

'Forty minutes at the most,' said the Doctor firmly. His wife gave him one of those enquiring looks that only human wives can give. We began walking across the meadow, down the road to where the path across the fields leads up to the Church. The Doctor strode out ahead with his dog running alongside. The three women, his wife, a friend and the Rector's wife, were soon deep in conversation. I was soon deep in mud, for the track had been churned up in places where various vehicles had been. The Rector fell behind and tried to encourage me to hurry. I decided to take my time and explore.

'Come on, Dennis,' shouted the Rector. The Doctor turned round. He has the same name as me. However, it had the desired effect, as the party, which had become somewhat separated, again came together. We crossed the final field, which ends on the road that leads up to the Church. This is quite a pull, and I had to suffer the same old joke from some folk coming down the hill, about wearing down my legs.

'We've made good time,' said the Rector. 'Can we go another

way back?'

'Oh, yes, we can go through the wood,' said the Doctor as we walked and slithered down the path that leads from the Churchyard to the fields below. Instead of going on to Hanbury Wood, we turned left on to the path through the wood, which was to take us back to the track across the meadow. The start was far from promising. The humans made heavy weather of getting over the fence. I simply slipped underneath into six inches of mud.

'It will be different when we get to the top,' said the Doctor enthusiastically. It was. The mud was a foot deep. Walking up this path, which would have been excellent for the downhill ski-run, if skis ran on mud instead of snow, we all made slow progress, except for the Doctor's dog, whose longer legs helped him to bound up, and the Doctor, who seemed to be propelled upwards by his own determined cheerfulness. The ladies were quite out of breath and the Rector was again at the rear, seeking to exhort me to greater efforts.

'Oh look. Snowdrops!' said one of the ladies. Gasps of enthusiasm followed, which I thought were rather overdone for such a small clump.

We continued to climb upwards. When we were on the top, the going was no easier. My black and tan fur was beginning to turn into a uniform khaki. The ladies, who were wearing boots, were hopping around as if their footwear was covered with a none too appetising chocolate blancmange. The Rector, who was wearing stout walking shoes, looked as if he wasn't. Going down the other side was just as hazardous. At last, we were back in the field and proceeding along the track, which was only normally muddy.

The Doctor raced back to the car. Our forty-minute walk was completed in ninety minutes. By the time I reached the edge of the road, the car was there, ready and waiting. Funnily enough, no one was keen to have me on his, or her, lap, but the words, 'Oh Dennis!' on this occasion, were not directed at me.

Holiday Opportunities

HOLIDAY TIME MEANS members of the family coming home to the Rectory. It's always part of my job to dash up and welcome them. They always appear with large holdalls and suitcases. Can they be crammed full of lovely things to eat? I wonder, as I make an excited exploratory sniff. They never are. Most of the contents end up in the washing machine. I've never cared much for washing machines. They make funny noises and ominous whirring sounds that send me straight back into my basket.

However, there is one thing in the kitchen I am interested in. It's the fridge. The door is normally kept firmly shut and it is usually only opened up around meal times. Holidays are different. When John, the little master, is home (actually he's the tallest one of the family), he seems to have to make frequent trips to the fridge. His capacity to consume milk and his love of making cheese sandwiches are quite awesome to a dog like me, who is limited to one or two meals. He says he has to make up for the frugal meals on offer at his boarding school.

On one of his trips to the fridge, I noticed that the remains of the Sunday joint – a succulent piece of roast beef – was on a plate on the lowest shelf. However, it might as well have been on the moon, as far as I was concerned, as each time he went to the fridge, the door slammed shut with a very definite bang. Then it happened. After one visit, there was no bang, but a gentle tap. I could hardly believe my ears or my luck. As little master left to go into the sitting room, with another glass of milk, and a sandwich, I made for the fridge. The door was not shut.

Quickly, I pushed my nose in and, with the rest of my body, I pushed hard on the door, which swung open, to reveal a dog's Aladdin's Cave. There was more here than the joint; there were sausages, bacon, cheese, part of a pork pie, the remains of a liver casserole and more. If there had been time, I might have written a hymn – 'Refrigerator the golden, with beef and cutlets blest'. But there was no time to go on to 'What joys beyond compare'. I pulled the joint out and was soon bolting it down. No wonder they keep treasures like this locked away – which is very selfish of them. Time for reflection was short. A shout of 'DENNIS!' heralded the return of little master.

There was no going back, not that there was much to put back as far as the joint was concerned. We confronted one another. I made my usual show of defiance, rolled my eyes, bared my teeth and did my best to make a threatening growl. Little master was unimpressed. He picked up a jug of water and threw it over me as I escaped into the garden.

There was no one there except the daffodils to salute my victory. Still, some things are worth suffering for, and that beef was most delicious.

Dennis in Disgrace

I KNOW I SHOULDN'T have done it. However, we all make mistakes sometimes, as the Rector says, and he ought to know. It all happened during the Easter holidays. The Rector's wife thought my diary would be improved by the addition of some illustrations. Now, drawing is not one of my talents. While my paws can cope with the keys on a typewriter, they are not made for holding pencils or paintbrushes. I know some humans can use their mouths, but by breeding and inclination, I have never gone in for holding sticks in my mouth. 'Let lesser breeds without the jaw', as the poet says, chase after sticks if they want to.

Anyhow, one of the teachers from St. Peter's came to draw me. The idea fascinated me and I kept trying to climb into her lap, to see how she was doing and to give her some encouragement. While she perfectly understood what I was about, the family kept shouting, 'Dennis!' and 'Look this way'.

Then, they wanted some action shots. If they thought they were going to get me interested by jumping up and down and shouting, 'Good Dog,' with set grins on their faces, I soon put them right. I am a hound of principle and never respond to bribes – except in the form of bones, cakes, all kinds of meat and certain kinds of biscuit.

One of the family scooped me up and carried me out into the garden. 'Look at the goldfish, Dennis.'

I ask you, where's the sense in that? Fish are totally boring, and only seem to be of interest to visiting cats. This stunning dialogue, taken straight from Janet and John books, continued – 'Walk this way. Turn round. Sit down. I said sit!'

If they had wanted one of those performing poodles, they shouldn't have gone in for dachshunds. I stretched out and yawned.

'That's it. Hold it.'

How can you hold a yawn? I'd had enough of this drawing business, and went back into my basket and closed my eyes. Let them all get on with it – that's my motto. Suddenly, I felt a hand on my basket. Biscuit thieves! After my last Bonio, hidden in the folds of the blanket. Instinctively, I grabbed the hand with my mouth.

There was a loud exclamation from the owner of the hand. I had bitten the artist. My popularity rating went to below zero. How was I to know she just wanted to adjust the angle of the basket, to get a better view of me?

I was in deep disgrace. Now, I know that Rectory dachshunds, like Rectors, are meant to be nice to everyone, and I certainly didn't mean to bite the hand that drew me. The artist was, in fact, most understanding, but the family said they were all deeply ashamed of me. Confession is said to be good for the soul, but my penance came later, with some long walks up and down the Dales of Derbyshire.

Will my diary be illustrated? You could say, 'I refuse to be drawn!'

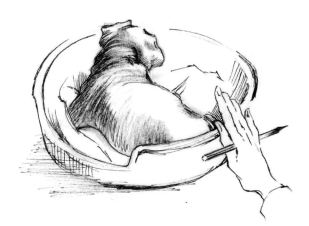

Dodging the Bandit

W E DON'T USUALLY go away in May; so, imagine my surprise when I saw the Rector packing the car. It happed this way because the Rector's wife had been given a one-term sabbatical, which I think is a kind of holiday, from King Edward's High School, where she teaches chemistry. Now, normally this packing is a tricky operation accompanied by half-muffled prayers as he wrestles with the cases and boxes, and things that won't go in to either. However, this time, all was sweetness and light. On the way backwards and forwards from the car, he actually found time to give me an encouraging pat.

'Packing for two is child's play,' he said. Two? I had seen my basket going in. Were we leaving the Rector's wife behind, as well as not taking the children? Maths never was a particularly strong subject with the Rector, as I have heard him say; so, three of us set off for Cornwall.

On the way, we spent a day in Worle, near Weston-super-Mare, with the Rector's mother. We went for a long walk out along Sand Point. It was something of a climb to reach the cliff path, but soon we were strolling along it, with the sea on either side. The Rector's wife was looking for wild flowers. She didn't have to do much looking – the place was covered with patches of bluebells and cowslips. I narrowly escaped a confrontation with a sort of terrier called Bandit. He looked the part too – wild eyes, drooling at the mouth, snarling and tugging at the lead.

'He's quite playful, really,' said Bandit's owner, but I was relieved to be out of the way before the extent of Bandit's playfulness was revealed. We arrived at the end of the Point. The sun was shining, so they sat on the seat, gazing at the sea, while I did my own exploration of some interesting holes and fascinating smells. It was a good walk and quite a change from the Worcester Road and the Ministry of Defence.

The next day, we arrived in Cornwall. Once out of the car, I went to the steps that lead up to the chalet where we always stay.

'Look, he's remembered. Clever boy!'

As we have spent nearly every summer holiday here since I was a pup, I hardly thought I needed such lavish praise. Instead of scooping me up and carrying me up the chalet steps, the Rector took me into the house next door. Yes, we were actually going to stay in a house. The week went very quickly. There were walks onto the cliffs where the sheep were grazing. There were walks along the coastal paths where sea pinks and primroses bloomed along with many other wild flowers, and walks across the rocky beach to explore little pools (l could never see the point of this as we have goldfish in our pond at home that you can look at with less than half the trouble).

We went on an outing to Tintagel, to see King Arthur's Castle. Mercifully, I was carried up and down the steep staircases which link together what's left of it. Below us raged the sea. The Rector went on about knights and 'letting loose the dogs of war'. This dog clung on firmly and was greatly reassured when we stopped playing at King Arthur. We crossed the sea in a boat once, when we went to Padstow and, from there, to Rock. It is a walk we always do when we are in Cornwall. You go up and down some dunes and follow the white stones, which take you across a golf course to St. Enodoc's Church. Golfers seem such impatient people and don't realise that each white stone has a particular interest for me.

'They are waiting to tee off, Dennis.'

Well, I wasn't stopping them, was I? We always carry our tea in a thermos flask and have no need to swing sticks around before drinking it. At last we arrived at the little Church, which, for hundreds of years, was almost completely buried in the sand. We sit on a little bench in the churchyard for our picnic. The Rector's wife opens the thermos and tea is certainly on. Nearby is the grave of a fellow-writer, one Sir John Betjeman, who wrote poetry. All is peaceful until some visitors approach us, obviously after our picnic. I try to keep them at bay, remembering King Arthur and the knights, and that Bandit. The Rector doesn't appreciate this. He thinks I am merely making a nuisance of myself. Still, it was a good holiday.

Vandals Strike Again

IT WAS A LOVELY MORNING, bright and fresh; my nostrils were quivering excitedly, in the expectation of all the various smells that were positively waiting to be investigated. I struggled to get down on the ground. My early morning walks often begin with the Rector carrying me away from the Rectory, as he complains I am too slow, when everyone is in a hurry. Frankly, I think they miss so much in all the rushing around. However, he put me down on the pavement in Old Coach Road. The path is fenced here so I am allowed to be free range. At 7.30 a.m., we meet few people, so I am at liberty to pursue my investigations in peace. The Rector looked across at the row of houses opposite, some of which have ravens moulded in the plasterwork.

'Memories of John Corbett and old Droitwich,' murmured the Rector. 'Did you know, Dennis, that John Corbett was the salt king, a man who did a lot for the people of this town, in the reign of Queen Victoria?'

However, I was too busy picking up the scent of some Labrador who had passed that way, much more recently than John Corbett. Dogs do not go in for nostalgia; we prefer the present and the immediate.

The grass in Witton playing fields looked fresh and inviting but nowadays there is no legal way through for dogs.

We came to the end of the path and turned into the Worcester Road, which was already buzzing and alive with cars. I was still allowed my freedom, with the Rector walking between me and the traffic. Suddenly, he shouted, 'Dennis! Wait!'

I stopped and looked round at him but he was looking at a sea of glass that was in front of us. As a much younger dog, I cut my paw in Dovedale once, on a broken bottle someone had thoughtlessly left in a field.

The Rector scooped me up and said, 'We can't have you going through that. The vandals have been at it again.'

There was a certain weariness in that last sentence. A whole panel of the bus shelter had been wilfully destroyed.

'What pleasure do they get in doing this sort of thing?' said the Rector. 'It's there for everyone's benefit.'

We returned to the Rectory. It was still a pleasant morning but somehow it seemed chillier. I climbed into my basket. 'What makes these vandals destroy things that are there for their benefit?' I wondered, as I absentmindedly chewed yet another hole in my blanket.

Fete Worse than Death

'SEASON OF GARDEN PARTIES and fetes worse than death', to quote the Rector, parodying somebody else, is now upon us. As the Rectory hound, I am always willing to do my share, so it was no surprise to me to be asked to open the Bible Society Fair. On these occasions, you always have to dress up, so I consented to wear a bright blue bow. The Rector's wife took me down the Worcester Road to the Methodist Church Hall. We walked along in the sunshine; but where were the cheering crowds? I asked myself. We entered the hall, where the stalls were arrayed with goods of all kinds. However, I thought it was rather tactless that there wasn't a doggie's stall with homemade chewers and chocolate biscuits and bowls of marrowbone trifles. The organiser called the gathering to order and I prepared to deliver my speech. But the Rector's wife decided to talk instead. This was a shame, as the company missed my sermon. Looking at the stall with the cuddly toys, my text was from Ecclesiastes 9:5 – '*A living dog is better than a dead lion.*'

My thoughts were interrupted as the people clapped politely when the Rector's wife finished her speech. A little girl came forward with a presentation but it turned out to be a basket of flowers. Well, I thought, they are bound to give me something; we made a tour of the stalls, buying an item from each. Surely, they were going to give me something. Then a man suggested we took tea. Things at last were looking up. The Rector scooped me up and carried me into the car, leaving behind tables groaning beneath cakes and biscuits and homemade jam. What a way for the Opener to be treated!

There I languished, thinking of all the terrible things that can happen to dogs when left for hours in cars. As it was, they were only away for about half an hour. Out they came, with all the things they had bought: bath salts, cakes, needlework and biros, but, as far as I could see, not a single Bible.

We set out for home via Dorset House, a pleasant home for elderly humans, where a Garden Party was in progress. Someone else had opened it and, like me, was wearing a collar but of a more ostentatious kind. Apparently, Mayors wear collars but there was no sign of a lead. I suppose it's because, as the Rector says, politicians always try to lead you by the nose.

Firm hands lifted me onto the lap of one of the residents. Appreciation at last. Expert stroking and lots of compliments. At last, I was getting the treatment due to a celebrity. Back at the Rectory, all sorts of preparations are going on. Instead of the Rector singing snatches of hymns, it's 'California, here I come'.

Barking at the Bishop

'A CAT MAY LOOK at a king, so why can't a dog bark at a Bishop?'
That's what I asked myself as I was bundled out into the back
garden.

It all happened one sunny afternoon in September, when a dog
likes to get his head down in the verandah, shaded by tomato plants
and baskets of apples and damsons. The Bishop, his wife and daughter
were coming to tea, so there was no peace for the wicked, or dogs.
The rector mowed the lawn and relieved the pond of yards of weeds,
slicks of slime, handfuls of muddy rotting leaves and a plastic bread-
bag, in between taking a wedding and putting the finishing touches to
a sermon about angels.

He expressed some surprise at the healthy state of Moby Dick and
the rest of the fish, which I thought showed a lack of faith in the efforts
I make to discourage presumptuous cats.

Daphne spent most of her morning at the Parish Centre. (I don't
get down there very often myself, though you could say I have made
my mark, witnessed, unfortunately, by one of the choirboys, who was
delighted for once to be in the position of being able to tell someone
else off.) Mary was busy baking and chatting to a school friend, and
delicious smells kept wafting from the kitchen.

By the time the Bishop arrived, we were all ready and I was looking
forward to a sausage-roll or two and the occasional ham sandwich,
with perhaps a scone with cream and jam. When tea was announced,
after what seemed an interminable length of time, I led the way into

the dining room and dutifully took up my place under the table.

Now, it says somewhere that, if you are invited to a feast, you should take the lowest place and the host will say, 'Friend, come up higher'.

I do not recall any translation containing the words, 'Get out of it!' I had no intention of complying with such an unreasonable request, uttered between clenched teeth. Then, as they appeared to have forgotten that even dogs are entitled to eat the crumbs that fell from the table, I decided to remind them. That was how I found myself suddenly, Lazarus-like, on the other side of the patio-window, looking in, while everyone else tucked into the tea.

It seems that a dog may look at a Bishop, but barking is strictly for the birds!

A Sponsored Walk

A N INVITATION ARRIVED from the Parents of St. Peter's School, asking the Rector's wife if she would start off a Sponsored Walk, to raise funds to promote health and safety. I heard her say, 'It starts at 10 o'clock in the morning. I think I shall take Dennis.'

I raised my head at the mention of my name. Why did I have to go? I was feeling perfectly healthy and completely safe, spread out on my rug in front of the fire. What is more, I wasn't asking anyone to sponsor me to do it.

The Rector's wife went on with mounting enthusiasm, 'He could wear his blue ribbon again, the one he wore to open the Bible Society Fair'.

Now, that had been on a warm summer afternoon, not a grey November morning.

Yes, it was a murky morning, and the Rector drove us round to St. Peter's for the start of the Sponsored Walk. We drove into the car park, which was almost empty. Where was the sound of happy children's laughter? The course had been optimistically marked out with tape; the walkers were expected to go round the field in laps of a quarter of a mile. It was so cold that the only lap I could think of, or be interested in, was to lap up a saucer of warm milk. The organisers had fallen down on this; none was provided.

'Come along, Dennis,' said the Rector's wife, giving a tug on the lead, to get me to the starting line. My nose was feeling as blue as the ribbon round my neck.

The Headmaster greeted us with a warm smile, which was the only thing that was warm, that morning. The grass was clammy under my paws, which kept sinking in the mud. There were only a few children and their parents present at the beginning but the Headmaster thought that more would be coming later in the day.

Soon we were off. The children got off to a brisk start, followed by the Rector's wife. 'Come on, Dennis,' she called, somewhat impatiently. I put an uncertain paw forward and set off very slowly through the mud. Did I really have to go all round that field? Very gingerly, I began to bring up the rear. Actually, I wasn't in the rear for very long because I soon heard the children who had set off at the beginning coming up behind me and then passing me, making encouraging noises, which I ignored. I had been lapped! Well, by now, I was just about round one side of the square. My bow had untied itself and was dragging behind in the mud. It unravelled, picking up bits of twig and rotting leaves in the process. It felt even colder…

'Come on, Dennis, you can't take ALL morning over one lap.'

THAT SETTLED IT. I could see no reason for going round the field, when you could cut across it. Ignoring the tape, I simply strode under it and staggered over the Finishing/Starting line, where the Rector's wife was waiting for me.

'Well done, Dennis. It's good to help people.'

'Yes,' I thought, 'and it's even better when people help dogs.'

The Rector arrived shortly afterwards and took us back to the Rectory in the car, where I was given a nice rub down with an old towel, and retired gratefully to my basket.

Christmas will soon be here. I wonder if anyone is organising a sponsored event to promote the health and safety of dogs.

Temptation, Turkey and Tinsel

THIS YEAR, YOUNG MASTER undertook the task of decorating the Christmas tree. While this took place, I was kept shut up in the kitchen. The season of goodwill clearly didn't apply to dogs. When the tree was ready, the Rector and his wife were invited in for the official switching on of the lights. That was my chance. The Rector's wife stopped making mince pies, opened the kitchen door, and I raced into the dining room, where the tree stood, beautifully decorated, although I would prefer to say tastefully.

'Oh, look, Dennis is attracted by the lights.' But I wasn't. The only lights that interest me are not hanging on trees.

'No, he's after the chocolate novelties.'

Firm hands picked me up and it was back to the kitchen, with the door firmly shut in my face. Like the chocolate novelties, I was foiled again.

This year, Christmas parcels were kept well out of my reach, so I couldn't help to open any. Actually, I did manage to open one parcel but it only contained the Rector's new stole, and he got the blame for leaving it on the floor.

By far the most interesting part of Christmas is the food. My curiosity was aroused when the Rector said we were to have the visiting preacher for Christmas Dinner. We usually have turkey. I wondered what cold slices of Hebrew Scholar would taste like. I never found out as he always kept a respectful distance from me.

An unexpected bonus came when the Rector was carving up the

turkey. The knife slipped, and a large piece of cooked ham, which formed part of the stuffing, fell at my feet. It was like manna from heaven! Being a pedigree and, therefore, to the manna born, I knew it was meant for me. However, just in case the family thought differently, I gave them a warning growl as I gulped it down.

'It will make him ill, eating all that.'

It did, but I reckon it was worth it.

It's All Right for Some

I LOOKED UP from my basket by the boiler in the kitchen, but the Rector's wife wasn't talking to me.

'It's all right for some; going off for two days' holiday, while I am still at school.'

'A retreat isn't exactly a holiday,' the Rector replied, 'though I must admit I am looking forward to doing some reading. But we shall be living quite simply.'

'Now, don't tell me you'll be practising mortification of the flesh; not with all those nuns to fuss over you.'

What did it mean? I am always very sensitive to changes. I like things to stay as they are.

'Dennis looks all apprehensive. Don't worry. Going on retreat is like going into kennels, only there's strictly no barking. Everyone keeps quiet for most of the time.'

'But Dennis has never been in kennels,' the Rector's wife reminded him.

The day came for the Rector to go off to stay with the Nuns at Malvern. In addition to my early morning walk at 7.50 a.m. along the canal, he also carried me up to the Ministry of Defence along the Worcester Road, and I walked back to the Rectory. With a farewell pat and a rub of my chest, he was off in the car.

I was on my own and no one to look after me. My retreat had begun. For the next two days, for long periods, I was left on my own. However, when, on two mornings running, I was dragged from my warm basket at 7 a.m., and made to walk a stretch of the Worcester Road, I felt the mortification of the flesh was beginning.

On Tuesday, Eleanor looked in, so I had a little bit of very acceptable fussing.

On Wednesday afternoon, the Rector returned and I was delighted to see him back. He seemed very lively as he bundled me into the car, to go over to Westlands, for a meeting at St. Richard's School. After the meeting, we went for a welcome walk along the canal. When the Rector's wife came home, she asked him how the Retreat had gone.

'It was very good. Each one of the guest rooms is named after a saint. Mine was St. Dennis.'

Dennis the Detective

WE HAD JUST FINISHED our Sunday lunch, in our separate places – the family in the dining room and I, as usual, shut up in the kitchen, when the phone went. This time, it wasn't a bride wanting to check on the hymns, nor was it a baptismal party who had forgotten the time. This time, it was something SERIOUS.

The bishop had been for a confirmation service, which was why we were having a late lunch. When he got in the car, to drive away from Dodderhill, he had put his pectoral cross on the roof of the car. Now, he said that it was missing.

'We must go and look at once,' declared the Rector's wife, as she put down the phone. The weather was decidedly uncertain, and I shivered, but there was no escape because the lead was put on and off we went to Dodderhill. When we got out, it was obvious it was going to rain, if not pour down.

The Rector's wife was not deterred, and she said, 'If we find it, it should result in a canonry at least.'

'That's all very well, but what's in it for the dogs?' I thought, as we looked round the area where the car was parked, and then set off down the drive of the school, where the refreshments (to which I had not been invited) had taken place after the Confirmation.

'The sleeping policemen could have dislodged it,' said the Rector.

I couldn't see any policemen, only some bumps in the road, which was an additional hazard, as far as I was concerned.

They raked around in the grass edges and I gave an occasional sniff.

By the time we reached the A38, it was raining, as they say, cats and dogs.

'I'll go and look in the church,' said the Rector hastily. 'Perhaps he was mistaken about the car roof.'

I made to go with him but the Rector's wife stood firm.

'We'll complete the circle. You go to the church and I'll come up and meet you.'

We started to walk down the A38. Cars splashed us as they hurtled by and, of course, there was no sign of the cross. We turned into the Church Lane, to go back to the church. I was tugging at the lead, being what they call a 'very soggy doggy'.

Then it happened. Something was gleaming in the road. IT WAS THE BISHOP'S CROSS.

The Rector's wife held it up in tremendous excitement. The chain had snapped but the cross with the diocesan coat of arms had been found.

'At last,' I thought, 'we can get back to the car.'

Both of us were completely soaked but this did not dampen her spirits.

'Well,' said the Rector, as we drove home, 'when Helen found the cross, they made her a saint.'

I have been called many things, but I don't think the Rector has ever called me a saint before. St. Dennis has a certain ring about it, though, and I recall passing through a village of that name, down in Cornwall. Anyway, it should be good for extra rations.

Thoughts of St. Augustine
and Corkey the Cat

HALF TERM MEANS visiting. First, we went off to Weston Super Mare, to visit the Rector's mother. After I had made my inspection of the bungalow and visited both the front and back gardens, I was rewarded with a dish of steak and kidney. Things were looking up.

We went for a stroll across the cliffs at Clevedon. It was a bright day and we all breathed in the bracing sea air. Our walk brought us to a pretty little churchyard – even on holiday we can't keep away from churches.

One of the monuments in the churchyard was to a vicar's wife. There was a lengthy description of all her good works, which the Rector somewhat tactlessly started to read aloud. To emphasise her good and useful life, the monument was in the form of a well to provide water for the flowers. I went for a little walk.

'No, Dennis! The *well* is for watering the flowers.'

Somewhat unceremoniously, I was dragged out of the churchyard. Sometimes, you would think they were ashamed of me.

The next day, we were off to the village of Trench in Shropshire. This time, we were visiting the Rector's wife's sister. Last time, they made quite a fuss of me. We went in through the front door, and, after the usual exchange of kisses, they all immediately started talking. However, they had thoughtfully left a dish of tasty morsels for me. I rapidly ate the lot, to show my gratitude.

'Dennis! He's eaten the cat's dinner,' said the Rector apologetically.

'Never mind,' said the Rector's sister-in-law, 'I can find some more for the cat. We call him Corkey because he keeps bobbing up.'

I looked around, but there was no sign of that cat. After lunch, we went out into the garden, to dig up some leeks. There, lurking beneath the bushes was a black and white cat. So, this was Corkey. Its eyes looked decidedly unfriendly. With its back arched and its fur rigid, I suppose it thought it could intimidate me. I gave a low growl. The cat hissed back, but did not move. I growled a little louder and moved closer. Then I started to bark and ran towards it. The cowardly animal turned and fled. You would think that, having been vanquished, it would have shown some respect to the victor. Instead, it merely sat on the fence, looking down at me with that same look of contempt in its eyes.

Well, what do you expect from a cat? What I didn't expect was a reprimand from the Rector's wife.

'Dennis! Corkey lives here. It's his garden.'

I could swear that that cat looked positively triumphant – but from a safe distance, of course.

On the way home in the car, the Rector murmured, 'Never mind, Dennis, remember the words of St. Augustine, *'Lord make me chased – but not yet.'*

What a Great Dane

WE WERE WALKING along the canal path, in the early morning, when suddenly a duck carrying a worm in her beak dashed across our path. In hot pursuit were two drakes. I just stood and looked. All that fuss over a worm.

'Come along, Dennis,' called the Rector. 'We've got a visitor coming today, and I think you'll be in for a surprise.'

Back at the Rectory, I wondered what it was going to be. The doorbell rang and, instead of going to answer it at once, the Rector put my lead back on again. We went to the door, and the Rector opened it. There stood Mr. Godfrey.

Well, I've seen plenty of vicars during our time at the Rectory, so another one wasn't really a surprise. However, bounding up behind him came Perry, a beautiful, honey-coloured Great Dane.

We stood facing one another in the hall. Frankly, I was rooted to the spot, craning my neck to look up at this fascinating creature. I could tell that I had made an impression on her, as well. She gazed down at me, her jowls positively drooling with saliva.

'Have you got a paper handkerchief, or something?' asked Mr. Godfrey.

'Some kitchen towelling would be better,' said the Rector. 'Do you think I can let Dennis off his lead?'

'I am sure you can,' said Mr. Godfrey. 'Perry may be large, but she is very gentle.'

We continued to gaze at one another in wonder. Then, suddenly, Perry leaped past me and bounded upstairs to the bedrooms. This, I thought, was very forward of her, I very rarely go upstairs, and am never allowed in the bedrooms. Mr. Godfrey called her back down again.

'She's a very inquisitive dog. She likes to do a full inspection,' said Mr. Godfrey.

'I can see that,' said the Rector. 'Would she like a run in the garden?'

'Let's see,' replied Mr. Godfrey. He called her and immediately she bounded out into the garden. I followed her to the door and concluded that it wasn't all that warm. Besides, they were about to have coffee, and where there's coffee, there's usually biscuits. If I were a drake and had the choice between the ducks and the worm, I'd go for the worm every time. All the same, that Perry is fascinating.

After coffee, the Rector said he'd go and see how Perry was. He looked round the garden but there was no sign of her. He looked over the hedge into our neighbour's garden, and there she was. He called out to her, but she thought this was a cue for the play to begin.

Mr. Godfrey joined the Rector in the garden, and, on one word of command, Perry was back. The Rector looked relieved.

'I was wondering how I was going to face the neighbours,' he said. 'Just imagine going round to their front door and saying, "Please can we have our Great Dane back?"'

Mr. Godfrey and the Rector continued their meeting. How they got on, I am not sure. However, that Perry is certainly a Great Dane.

Bank Holiday Exhaustion

'IT WILL BE NICE to have a rest at half-term,' said the Rector's wife, when she came in from school. The end result was a week of frantic activity, going from place to place in search of a rest. First of all, we went up to young master's College, near Uttoxeter, for Speech Day. I thought this was bound to be restful, especially when I heard the Rector say, 'I usually nod off on these occasions'.

Not a bit of it. No sooner had we arrived at Denstone than the Rector's wife suggested a walk beforehand. Off we went along the Churnett Railway track from Denstone, in the direction of Alton Towers. On either side, trees and shrubs were full of fresh green leaves and blossom. We walked through what seemed an open tunnel of May. The air was clear and I could smell a whole range of scents. We arrived back at the College in good time. Whether or not the Rector went to sleep during the speeches, I don't know, because I was left in the back of the car with a bowl of water and a biscuit.

Back in Droitwich with young master, the house became a laundry, but it was made clear my help was not needed. Bank Holiday Monday saw us on the bank of the canal. We walked from Oddingley to Dunhampstead. Clearly, everyone was having a holiday from banks, as we met no one except an enthusiastic jogger.

'Mad dogs and Englishmen...' sang the Rector.

On Wednesday, we went to Bakewell and took more walks. There was a notice, which read 'Keep your dog on a lead – Sheep'. The Rector dutifully complied. The whole flock were clearly waiting for this, as they started to follow us.

'Very Biblical,' laughed the Rector's wife.

I thought it was undignified, being seen off by a flock of sheep. The longest walk was along part of Lathill Dale. We walked between the dry-stone walls of a farm, then, suddenly, the path became steeper as we went down into the Dale itself. The water in the river was very clear. You could see the fish if you wanted to, but by now I was finding it quite hard just putting one paw in front of another.

Home again. Perhaps, now, the rest would begin. But no – we were off to the seaside, to visit the Rector's mother. We got out of the car and she came out to welcome us.

'Hallo, Mother. What would you like to do?'

'How about a nice walk?' she said.

I thought I was in luck when I saw these signs at Weston-Super-Mare saying 'No Dogs allowed on the beaches.'

'Don't worry,' said the Rector's mother, 'Dennis needn't be disappointed. There are other beaches where you can walk for miles.' And we did.

The half-term holiday ended, and it took me a week to recover.

The End of the Road

GETTING BACK REFRESHED from Cornwall, I resumed my daily duties. Every morning, whatever the weather, the Rector and I went for a walk along the canal bank in Vines Park. As the train to Birmingham passed by, the Rector would look out for his wife and wave, sometimes with me tucked under his other arm. More often, I was about my own affairs in the bushes. On our return to the car, we met a number of people; there was Charlie on his bike, heading for school, and Paul the organist always stopped for a little chat on his way to work, and without fail he asked after me. In the evenings, we would come back to Vines Park for a little walk across the wooden bridges. The Rector would then leave me in the car with my own thoughts while he went into St. Andrew's for Evening Prayer.

Another unexpected trip to the seaside happened when the Rector went to see his mother in Weston. The day was somewhat overcast but the rain kept off and we walked across the causeway which separates the Marina from the full force of the sea. Large puddles of seawater blocked the path and I felt like the Israelites did at the Red Sea. I stood and shivered until the Rector scooped me up and carried me over. We walked across quite a large expanse of beach but I was ready to go back to the car. In fact, I almost made it on my own, and the Rector was given a lecture by a passer-by on his lack of wisdom in allowing me off the lead, as I stood by myself on the edge of the kerb, by the traffic lights. Actually, he had been engrossed in conversation with his mother, and hadn't spotted my progress. I could see he was somewhat shaken.

At the Rectory, I continued my accustomed pattern of life, but something irresistible was beginning to take hold of me. Yes, I was slowing down considerably. Casual passers-by continued to make jokes about my little legs, linking this with my lack of progress. (If only they could have seen the way I dashed into that Loch on Arran.)

I wanted to say, 'It's not my legs – it's what manages them.'

Advent arrived, and the Rector was busy preparing his sermons on Hope, Judgement and all things being summed up in Christ. All things?

By now, walking was becoming a much greater effort, but I needed to walk. Another visit to the Vet's followed. When my name was called, I hid under the chair.

'It will be a day or two before we can expect any improvement,' said the Vet. 'It could be three days.'

Although the injection had been painless, I strode out of the Vet's with more speed than I had been able to muster for some time.

The three days passed. Dutifully, I continued my walks, but felt strongly drawn to my basket with the old blue blanket filled with the holes I have made. On Friday evening, I missed the arrival of the Rector's son and his wife, and remained where I was. On Saturday morning, I almost missed out on the bacon from the breakfast table, but the smell was too compelling and I gratefully gobbled up the succulent scraps.

The Rector's wife took me for my Sunday morning walk through St. Mary's Churchyard. It was hard going, but I managed most of it, with a little help from the Rector's wife. All the same, I was grateful to get back to my basket. There I remained, with this strange sense of drifting. After lunch, the Rector set off for Bromsgrove, where he was taking part in a Scout Carol Service. He had been asked to preach on 'Animals'! Before he left, he came over to me and I felt his hands giving me a reassuring stroke and pat.

'You'll be all right, Dennis!'

When he'd gone and his son and his wife, who had been staying with us for the weekend, had left, I started to get out of my basket and make for the kitchen door. I needed to go into the garden. The Rector's wife, sensing this and seeing my difficulty, picked me up in her arms – ever so gently – and carried me down to the bottom of the garden by the old damson tree. My legs were very shaky, but I managed to get some relief and then just stood there. She went back to the kitchen, leaving me to follow when I was ready, as I always did. This time, there was no need. I simply stood under the damson tree in the garden I know so well. In my younger days, I have chased cats away from the pond where the goldfish are. I know every tree and bush, with its own particular smell. Here I have buried delicious bones, like St. Paul's preaching, both in season and out of season.

But all these things are passing, as they must. The Master is calling. Another garden? 'You'll be all right, Dennis!'

Epilogue

Dennis died on Sunday, 10th December, in the garden at the Rectory.

He had been part of the family for nearly twelve years, since we saw him as one of a litter of puppies – in the Police House at Alvechurch.

While we were his owners, we never possessed him. He was a pet, but not a toy, and his capacity to make people laugh never detracted from his dignity. In the pages of the magazine, his activities have been expressed through a human voice, but he was always his own dog. He gave us great joy.

Sadly, at this time of year in particular, many dogs are abandoned, having lost their novelty value. Dog ownership is a privilege, which carries responsibilities.
C.S.

> *He prayeth best, who loveth best*
> *All things, both great and small;*
> *For the dear God who loveth us,*
> *He made and loveth all.*
>
> Samuel Taylor Coleridge.

Our house seemed so empty after Dennis died. A few months later, unbeknown to me, Daphne saw a dachshund advertised in *The Birmingham Post* and made some enquiries.

As a result, we found ourselves at a house in Erdington, looking down at a longhaired miniature dachshund puppy of only a few weeks. The name seemed bigger than he was. Indeed, when we took him to the vet, the vet asked, 'What on earth is that?'

We were soon to find out, as Jubilee started to find his feet in our house and explore the opportunities open to a rectory hound.

Walking on the Water

WHAT A LOT HAS HAPPENED since last year, when the only world I knew was my basket in a small house in Erdington. I have learned to do so many things. Why, I can even walk on water – well almost.

One very cold morning, I went out into the garden for ball practice. The Rector throws a tennis ball and we both chase after it. If I get it first, I try to keep it and he has to chase me to get it back. We were doing this when I spotted a blackbird cheekily standing on the edge of our pond.

I wasn't going to stand for that. I dropped the ball and ran straight at that bird. As I drew near, he flew across the pond. Without hesitating, I followed, running over the goldfish beneath my feet

'Look out, Jubilee! It's not safe,' shouted the Rector.

However, I got over quite safely. I would have walked back again, but the Rector scooped me up and breathlessly carried me into the house. I thought he might be jealous because I don't think he's ever walked on water.

In the late afternoon, I went out into the garden again. It was a little warmer, so I ran to the pond, to have another go at walking on water. Suddenly, I found myself sinking into the stuff. It was everywhere; in my ears, in my mouth, up my nose, and my lovely fur was entwined with weed.

The Rector came out to look for me, but he didn't look into the pond, and I was too breathless to give even a whimper. He went back to the house, shouting, 'Jubilee!' Somehow, I dragged myself out, determined in future to leave the pond to the goldfish. I arrived at the back door, which was shut, and I shivered.

Fortunately, it was opened a few minutes later. The Rector took one look, went back into the kitchen and found a big towel. He wrapped me up in it.

Soon he was rubbing me dry and putting me down on a rug in front of the gas fire in the snug.

'Just remember, you're a miniature long-haired dachshund, not a dog-fish', he said.

But I didn't mind. I stretched out a little more, to let the fire toast my tummy.

Proud of Myself

IT WAS WHITSUNDAY MORNING when I received my white rosette 'Highly Commended'.

Edwin from the Dog Training Club delivered it to the Rector at St. Peter's. I didn't know about this until the Rector and his wife returned to the car, where I had been left in the car park during the early morning Service. Tongues of fire for the Apostles and a white rosette for me!

In celebration, I was given a run across the cricket field. Greeting other dogs, rolling over and over, and stopping to sniff at interesting places, I enjoyed my triumph. The Rector's wife came with me while the Rector drove the car round to Lyttleton Road, to pick us up.

I have had a busy month. There have been parishioners to visit, homes to inspect, and now I know what guinea pigs are.

I first saw these being fed, outside in the sunshine, at St. Peter's School. Some girls had carried them out of their cages and put them on some tree stumps, which served as stools for the children. What do guinea pigs do? I wondered. I leaped up to take a closer look at the little creatures. Laughingly, the girls pushed me down. Obviously, they didn't know that I was highly commended, but I still permitted them to tickle my tummy. What did the guinea pigs do? They twitched. At least, ducks run away, squawking, pretending to be frightened when I chase them back to the pond. The birds that land on our lawn take off when I approach; but these silly guinea pigs just twitched. The Rector tugged at my lead and said it was time to go. I still had hopes of getting the guinea pigs to do something.

'What was he highly commended for?' asked one of the girls, when the Rector told them about my rosette. 'For obedience,' said the Rector, giving the lead another tug, and leading me away.

It hasn't all been work. This month, we've had some lovely walks. The bluebells in Martin Stanley Park, and carpets of them in Trench Woods, have been visited. The blossom this year, they say, has been magnificent.

As I ran along the towpath at Oddingley, there was cow parsley on one side, and trees and hedgerows covered in white blossom on the other. Can it be that the whole countryside has been 'Highly Commended'?

Angels

THESE COLD FROSTY MORNINGS are no problem to me. Protected by my long furry coat, I bound across St. Peter's Fields. Exciting smells are sharpened up by the frost; while the leaves beneath my paws crackle (the Rector says it must be like walking through corn flakes).

Walks can provide other delights. Going through Trench Woods, I suddenly saw in front of me a plump pheasant. Naturally, I gave chase and, as I drew near, I saw that the bushes were full of pheasants. They all scattered in different directions. This was much more satisfying than the squirrels, who simply scamper up the nearest tree. The Rector and his wife caught up with me.

'We don't want to be had up for poaching,' he said.

'Yes,' said his wife, 'just imagine being hauled up before the magistrate and discovering you were standing before a member of the congregation!'

By now, the pheasants had retreated and we continued our walk.

'One day, Jubilee, those pheasants may get their own back on you,' said the Rector.

Some days later, I was in St. Nicholas' Church. Nicola, who had her leg in plaster, held me on her lap while, over tea, the Rector and his wife were talking to members of the congregation. Suddenly, I became aware of a strange figure beside me. It was all in white and had enormous wings. Could it be some kind of pheasant, come to seek revenge? Its upturned hand certainly looked threatening. I began to bark. Everyone looked round. Nicola tried to calm me down.

'It's only an angel, Jubilee,' said the Rector. 'You don't have to bark at angels.'

'That's strange,' I thought. 'Haven't I heard them singing, "Bark! The Herald Angels Sing"?'

What were the dogs doing while the shepherds kept watch over their flocks by night? I wouldn't be a bit surprised if they didn't give those angels a bit of a welcoming bark – not like that cat in the picture they've got in the Sacred Heart. An enormous angel appears to Mary, while the cat remains curled up and totally uninterested; but that's the difference between cats and dogs.

If I could talk, I could pass this idea on to the Rector. He might make use of it in his Christmas sermon.

Pastoral Duties

WE MOVED TO PENSNETT, just outside Dudley. The church, St. Mark's, is known locally as the Cathedral of the Black Country. The Vicarage stands next to it, at the foot of Barrow Hill. Just as the Rector, now the Vicar, has to learn about his new parish and its people, with their very distinctive way of talking, so I must discover what my new job entails, so to speak.

Among my duties at the Vicarage is the important task of welcoming. Some days this begins quite early. We walk through the coppice and across the park to High Oak, where the Vicar's wife catches the 7.12 a.m. bus. On the way back, the Vicar and I go past the school. Sometimes we see Margaret, our school's caretaker, and she gets the first welcome of the day, but she can't stay long. I think she has quite a lot of pups of her own to clean up after.

The last part of the walk takes us back through the churchyard. If I'm lucky, I see a familiar figure at the top of the steps that lead to the Vicarage. We can see Jamie, the paperboy, from some way off, as he wears a bright yellow waterproof and an even brighter smile. He bends down to ruffle my fur. We have a great game as I dodge backwards and forwards.

The other day, we enjoyed the game so much, that he forgot to put the newspaper through the letterbox. The Vicar says I'll make him late for school one of these days. Somehow, I don't think he'd mind too much!

I have nothing against Education. Indeed, it was my pleasure to welcome and to encourage those who came to our Education Sunday exhibition in the Church. But my main concern is the Vicarage. Here I welcome all-comers. The post-man is a little wary of me and I have to admit that I'm still quite suspicious of the milk-float, when I hear it grumbling its way up the lane with its headlights glaring. It comes right up the drive, without so much as by your leave, and then, just as suddenly, backs out noisily to disturb the rest of the parish.

Sometimes, important people come to the Vicarage, such as Churchwardens and the Secretary of the P.C.C., to discuss matters of policy. Others come to see the Vicar about their wedding, or the baptism of their children. Some come because they have something worrying them, or feel very sad. But I believe they all feel much better, when they touch my fur and give me a friendly stroke. I get great satisfaction from this. I think it's something of a mystery to the Vicar why this should be so.

But, then, he says that some people only come to touch him for money!

Bagging a Ghost

'AM YOU THE VICAR then?' the boy asked, as we came across him and his friends trying out the strength of the lampposts in Vicarage Lane.

'That's right,' said the Vicar, 'and this is Jubilee. Like you, he has an interest in lampposts.'

They laughed, but a little uneasily, I thought. Wanting to change the subject, one of them then asked, 'Have you ever seen a ghost?'

'No,' answered the Vicar, 'never.'

'But they say that there are ghosts up there,' the boy went on; pointing up the lane in the direction we had just come from.

'Yeah,' said another, 'There's the ghost of the man who was working on y our roof. He fell off and yer can see 'im at midnight all mangled up.'

'Well, I've never seen anything and the Vicar who was here for over twenty years never saw anything either,' replied the Vicar. 'Now, while you look for ghosts, I must go and look for my wife. Her bus should have arrived by now.'

After giving me a pat or two, the children disappeared into the darkness and we went to wait for the Vicar's wife on the seat at the War Memorial.

A few days later, we were out for our early morning walk in the Coppice. It was a dark, dreary morning and there was a bit of a wind blowing. Suddenly, I heard a strange sound and stopped dead in my tracks. There, in front of us, was a very mangled shape indeed. It was a horrible white colour, and had long, thin arms, and claw-like fingers that seemed to be struggling to reach us. Even the Vicar looked apprehensive as the thing continued to writhe. The darkness lifted a little and, as it did, the Vicar began to laugh.

'Look Jubilee!' he exclaimed, 'It's only an old white plastic bag caught in the bushes. Come on.'

He gave my lead a tug but I still wasn't keen to move. When we lived in Droitwich we used to walk through the park, and the park-keeper used to walk round with a black plastic sack. 'To collect rubbish,' was the reason he gave, and he would wave it in my direction. Many a time the Vicar had to chase after me as I rushed across the children's playground to escape. This time I could not run away.

'I think there could be a sermon in that plastic bag,' said the Vicar.

'Just as long as there's not a ghost in it!' I thought to myself, still pulling at my lead.

Some time after this, I heard the vicar tell someone that the first man to be buried in the churchyard was the man who had fallen off the Vicarage roof.

Reading the Signs

'**B**UT HOW DOES GOD get in touch?' asked an earnest voice from the study. 'How do we know, when we can't see him?' the voice went on.

I was on the other side of the study door and anxious to join in, so I started scratching at the door. This had the desired effect of getting the door open but an exasperated Vicar emerged and, bundling me up in his arms, somewhat unceremoniously, I thought, took me into the kitchen and said to his wife. 'I am trying to have a serious discussion and I can't have Jubilee disturbing us.'

'Well, I am trying seriously to make you all a cup of coffee,' she replied, 'but you can leave Jubilee here.'

So there I was, banished to my basket in the kitchen, and I only wanted to be friendly. I am always interested when people call at the Vicarage.

Our first visitor is usually Jamie, who comes with the newspaper. I rush out to greet him and I am always rewarded by some expert stroking and tickling. One snowy morning, he had not arrived by the time we had to set out for the bus stop. The Vicar's wife, for five days of the week, catches a bus at High Oak, just after 7 a.m. The Vicar and I go with her and then walk back through the Coppice. In the snow and ice, it is quite an expedition. So far, we have always made it but, in the snow and ice, we need extra time – at least they do. I scamper through the snow and, with my four legs, have no difficulty at all in remaining upright.

Returning from the bus stop, there was no sign of Jamie. He had obviously forgotten me this morning. The Vicar laughed and said, 'He hasn't forgotten you. Look!'

There, written in the snow, was 'Hi Jubi!'

I rushed up the drive to take a closer look. The Vicar went on thinking out aloud.

'I wish this had happened before our discussion group. God can always reach us somehow but we have to learn how to read the signs.

'Hi, Jamie! And thank you, God.'

Irish Botany Lesson

'W'HEN IRISH EYES ARE SMILING,' sang the Vicar, as he drove the car onto the ferry at Cairn Ryan.

I think he wanted to give the impression that going across the sea to Ireland was something we do every day. It was our first visit and for me it was the first time I had been on a car ferry. When you go to the Isles of Scilly, the car is left behind.

We found ourselves in what looked like a large underground car park, with all the cars packed closely together. The Vicar and his wife got out with some luggage they thought might be useful on the voyage.

'Perhaps we could leave Jubilee in the car?' said the Vicar.

I was not having that; I had heard them talk about these 'roll-on and roll-off ferries.' Suppose our car decided to roll off, while they were on deck enjoying themselves. I barked loudly in protest.

'Of course, we wouldn't leave you,' said the Vicar's wife, scooping me up under one arm while holding the bag with the thermos flask in the other. 'At least, I wouldn't!' She gave the Vicar a hard stare.

Soon I found myself on deck, exploring most of the facilities provided by P & O. The crossing went so smoothly that the Vicar forgot all about taking seasickness pills and refusing food, and went to the restaurant for an Ulster fry.

On arriving in Ireland, the Vicar decided we should go to the Giant's Causeway as that was fairly near. This was somewhat disappointing, as the Giant wasn't there. He'd just left his boot and piles of old rocks that the Vicar's wife enthused over. Apparently, they are geologically very important but I was not impressed. However, in a manner of speaking, l did leave my own little mark on some of them.

It was time for us to set out for our cottage. The Vicar's wife pointed out that there was on the map a reasonably straight road. This was not exciting enough for the Vicar, who claimed we could go by a more interesting route and see some picturesque churches and castles on the way.

I don't think we saw many of these, though we did find ourselves exploring parts of the Irish network of roads that even the Irish had forgotten about. When we reached a large austere building with steep walls and watchtowers labelled the Maze Prison, the Vicar's wife had had enough and suggested we just concentrated on finding the cottage.

About an hour later, we arrived at the place where the cottage was. We had been told it was called Honeysuckle Cottage. In the lane, there were a number of cottages but none of them was called this. There was no one around to ask. After the Vicar had tried one gate and been confronted by a far from welcoming dog, he decided that the best way would be to try the key we had been given in all the different doors. Whichever one it opened must be the cottage we had hired. He suggested his wife do this while he attended to the car, since the lane was quite narrow.

'I'll try this one first,' she said. 'It's got roses round the door.'

Ignoring the Vicar's protest that it should be honeysuckle, she put the key in the lock.

Like Cinderella, in one of the Vicar's pantomimes, she called out in triumph, 'It fits!' With that, we all went inside the cottage that was to be our home while we were in Ireland.

What a Friend We Have in Jesus

'WHAT A FRIEND we have in Jesus,' said the Vicar. 'That hymn was written here; it says so in the guide-book. The clock in the town square plays it on the hour.'

I looked up from my basket by the fireplace in our cottage in Banbridge, Northern Ireland. By now, we had settled well into our holiday home. I was becoming used to the routine. The Vicar and his wife would look up places in the various guidebooks; we would set out in the car to find them, and then a long walk would follow.

These usually turned out longer than expected, partly because the Vicar can never quite trust the guidebook to be entirely accurate and partly because he can't resist short cuts. He may seek to inspire but it's the rest of us who are left to perspire, as we go that extra mile the Bible talks about. However, the countryside is very attractive. The Mountains of Mourne really do sweep down to the sea. We know; we have tried it.

At Rostrevor, we climbed a mountain track to a large boulder that was something of a local landmark. Not content with this, the vicar insisted that we climbed even higher to get an even more dramatic view of the coast below and the Irish Sea. He was sure that there would be a path down. He had seen it on the map. Seeing things on a map and finding them on the ground are two different exercises.

The Vicar's wife sat down with me on a grassy mound, while the Vicar went to find the path down. He came back to tell us that he could see a track that the sheep used, so, presumably, that led to a path.

His wife was determined not to go back the way we'd come, as she considered it far too steep, and, what if one of us broke a leg? The Vicar said that he hadn't seen any sheep with a broken leg on this new path. We set off down the hillside. At first, the track was clear. It was steep but they could stand upright. With my four legs, there wasn't any problem!

Suddenly, the going became much rougher. The grass ended abruptly. Shale replaced the turf. To the left of us, the hillside was on fire. We felt the shale give way under our feet. We had started a mini-landslide.

Instead of going straight down, we tried traversing. We didn't seem to slip quite so much or quite so fast.

'We must make for that fence alongside that plantation of trees; at least we can hold onto that,' said the Vicar, slithering down another few feet.

By this time, I was the only one standing completely upright. The Vicar's wife was progressing downwards in a sitting position, making threats about never again going on anything so ridiculous.

'Here's the fence,' shouted the Vicar, 'and look, here's the stile. I knew we must be on the right path.'

I scrambled through. They climbed over and we made our way through the forest and to the car. That was why, back in my basket, I thought there must be a lot of truth in that hymn.

Hair Apparent

THERE'S NOTHING like a really good brush and comb!
After my morning walk, I look forward to feeling the prongs of
the comb on my chest, and it's a relief to have bits of grass and twigs
removed from my fur. However, I am not so keen when they pull at
my fur, in an attempt to remove knots and tangles, and I definitely
dislike being squirted from a can labelled 'flea spray'.

One Saturday, I found out how humans cope with their fur. Though
they have a lot less, they make much more fuss. The Vicar's wife took
me with her to the hairdressers. Looking round, I thought they must
have been having a lot of trouble with their fleas for one lady had her
head down in a sink, another was sitting under a large cone called a
drier and another was having bits of her hair cut off. New smells came
from opened bottles and drying towels. The whole scene was presided
over by Rita and Joyce, two cheerful and capable ladies bustling around
with their assistant Mandy to attend to the needs of customers and
exchanging views of what was going on in the village. They had
obviously been working so hard that part of the ceiling had fallen in!

They made me very welcome, and soon got to work on the Vicar's
wife. Someone suggested that I might like my fur trimmed because of
the heat. I hid under a chair. I wasn't having any scissors near me.
Besides, the Vet had said that my fur kept me warm in winter, and, in
the summer, protected my sensitive skin from the strong rays of the
sun.

I didn't stay under the chair for very long, as I recognised the voice
of the Vicar. 'What was he doing here?' I wondered.

'Can you fit me in?' he asked. 'I must look tidy for the weddings this afternoon.'

'I should think so,' answered Rita. 'What do you think of our ceiling?'

The Vicar looked up at the gaping hole, the crumbling plaster and the bare lathes.

'Oh dear!' he sighed, and added, for some obscure reason, 'The lath shall be first.' With that, the Vicar was led to a vacant chair and had an overall wrapped round him.

'Do you think we could have an appeal for our roof?' asked Rita.

'Perhaps we could have a joint appeal,' suggested the Vicar. 'We've got dry rot in the Church's... and I mean in the roof, not the pulpit.'

'I never said a word,' responded Rita, picking up a pair of shiny scissors. 'The difference is: they'll give to your appeal. We shall have to fend for ourselves.'

'Which I am sure you do very well,' said the Vicar, looking nervously at the scissors as if recalling what happened to Samson.

I sat by the Vicar's chair. The scissors flashed as Rita began to cut away at the Vicar's hair. The air became thick with hairs, as grey and white locks started to rain down on me. Having quite enough of my own – and of far better quality and colour, I started to move out of the way. I am quite content to be the Vicarage hound without being the hair apparent as well!

Love and the Lap-lander

ON FEBRUARY 14TH, you will be remembering St. Valentine's, but for me the Patron Saint of Love struck before Christmas. It was a cold but not unpleasant day as we walked on Highgate Common. I love to feel the springy turf of the open common beneath my paws and the crackle of frosted leaves as we explore the wooded areas. For the Vicar and his wife it is the views that get them: trees with their branches outlined by the frost, changing skies that light up and join the landscape, the wide expanse of grassland and gorse and the glimpses of frozen pools as we go down woodland paths. But for me, it's the smells.

We were just about to emerge from a small copse into open ground, when I became aware of a fascinating odour. I felt the ground shake. Into view came a honey-coloured Labrador. She was beautiful.

'A Marilyn Monroe of the canine world,' said the Vicar, remembering his younger days.

The Labrador looked down at me with longing eyes and drooling with desire. Suddenly, the silence was broken with breathless panting – not from the Labrador, but from her owner.

'Don't let him near her! She's fourteen days into it and desperate,' he shouted.

Looking at me, the Vicar said, 'She must be – but we haven't brought a ladder with us!'

Reluctantly, the Labrador was led away and we continued our walk. Soon it would be Christmas, and who could say what Santa Claus might bring?

In the event, four dogs came to visit us over the Christmas holiday. We get on quite well, when they remember that the vicarage and its garden are my territory, and stick to eating their own food.

We also had a number of human visitors but I think the best party was when the Servers came. They played various games and didn't seem to mind when I tried to join in. What I liked best was when they took it in turns to stroke me and let me stretch out on their laps. As their gentle hands caressed me, I thought, 'Well, I may not be very effective as a Labrador but I make a wonderful lap-lander!'

Revivalist Meeting at Old Folk's Home

'JESUS CHRIST is risen today, alleluia!'

'All right for some,' I thought, as I lay on the back seat of the car parked outside one of our residential homes, trying to ignore a black cat staring at me from the window. The Vicar and Carol, the curate, had gone inside to conduct a service for Holy Week and Easter. I had wanted to go in with them and made this plain by giving a good bark. The Vicar insisted that I stay in the car. It was then that I saw that cat. The creature looked so smug, as if to say, 'This is my house and you're not coming in, so there!'

Actually, it made no noise at all but I could tell what it was thinking. I barked even louder. It made no difference. The Vicar simply slammed the car door.

Half an hour later, the Vicar returned to let me out. I was going inside. As we walked up to the front door, the cat vanished. However, I knew he would be in there somewhere.

As I entered the lounge, I was met with expressions of welcome from the residents. They were all sitting in comfortable chairs. Some were asleep but I couldn't rest. That cat was lurking nearby; I saw a dark shape underneath a chair. I ran across to investigate. As I did so, a hand reached down to me.

The owner of the hand spoke, 'What a lovely little dog!'

She gave me a lovely stroke. I hoped that cat was looking. Soon, I began to forget about him as I did a tour of the residents. Each one said something complimentary. Some gave my fur a stroke while others tickled my tummy. Even those who had slumbered through the Vicar's talk woke up.

'Well,' said Carol, 'the dog is getting a better response than us. Jubilee's bringing everyone to life!'

I would like to have said, 'That's what Easter's all about.'

Why do human beings think that you can only reach people by talking to them? Perhaps that's why our Heavenly Father made us dogs?

Such deep thoughts made me forget about the cat entirely – at least for the time being. Back at the vicarage, I crept into my basket. All this parish visiting quite takes it out of a dog. I closed my eyes and looked forward to the time when I would be in a comfortable chair, basking in the sun, on the Isles of Scilly.

Star Prize to Carol, the Curate

THERE WAS GREAT excitement, as we set out for my Saturday morning walk through the Coppice. People were carrying tables and chairs out of the church. Others were sorting out boxes. A lady was ironing away purposefully, as games, groceries, bottles and mysterious packages were all taken to their rightful place. It was the day of the Garden Party.

'Where are the hot dogs?' somebody asked.

'I can only see one,' someone else replied, pointing at me. 'But he is a sausage dog!'

I gave him a hard stare. If I could speak, I would have replied, 'I am actually a long-haired, miniature dachshund.'

The Vicar gave a tug on my lead. He was anxious to begin our daily circuit, down through the churchyard, along the old railway track, across the field, up the steps and back down the lane.

'The sooner we get round, the sooner I can get back to help,' said the Vicar.

Soon we were crossing the field, where the horses were grazing, or lying down in the early morning sun. Birds were flying around, pretending to be busy. I explored the long grass, leaving the Vicar muttering away to himself about a 'fete worse than death'.

After all the rain we have been having, it was good to feel the sun on my fur once more. Back at the church, the pace had hotted up, as each of the stalls started to take shape. The Vicar was invited to put his head through the hole that replaced the head of a giant clown, just to try it out. Having seen a large bucket of water nearby and a pile of sponges, the Vicar – somewhat unsportingly – declined the invitation, saying that he and his wife were looking after the hoop-la. I ran round the stalls, barking encouragement.

In the afternoon, as the weather warmed up, so did the people. I was kept very busy giving them a welcome. While it seemed no one was going to ring one of the prizes, they got sweets for having a go and, if they were very lucky, I allowed them to give me a pat, or to tickle my tummy.

Carol, the curate, arrived and asked, 'If I get a hoop round the Vicar, do I win him?'

A small crowd gathered as Carol prepared to throw. She held the hoop in her hand, took careful aim and, with a flick of the wrist – the hoop sailed into the air, missed the Vicar and landed completely over the star prize!

It was a great moment, but only the first of many, because Carol says I can go and visit Becky, her delightful mongrel dog, when they move to Chadsmoor.

Guard Dog Duty

WE HAD JUST COME BACK from the Isles of Scilly, and with all that jumping about from boat to boat and the long drive back from Penzance, more than one of us was dog-tired. It was strange at first, to be coming back to our new vicarage, instead of the Rectory in Worcester Road, the Vicar, as I must now call him, wondered if we had had any unwelcome visitors. I did a quick tour of the house and garden but there were no unfamiliar or suspicious smells. All was well.

The next day was Sunday, so it was 'all systems go', but by the afternoon, we were ready for a rest before the Evening Service. Suddenly, the Vicar shouted that there was someone at the door, although the bell had not rung. I ran downstairs, barking furiously. The Vicar's wife was behind me. She opened the door but there was no one there.

'What's all that fuss for, Jubilee? You and the Vicar must be hearing things!' On Monday morning, the Vicar went into his study – it is by the front door – he came out very quickly.

'We have a problem,' he said. 'Somebody has tried to break in.'

The Vicar's wife and I went running into the study. The Vicar showed us the broken glass and the hole that had been made with a screwdriver, or something similar. Later, when the police arrived, they agreed that someone had tried to break in.

'Usually, they get further than this,' said the policeman. 'Something must have disturbed them.'

'Something!' I thought to myself. 'You mean someone, someone who came round on Sunday afternoon and who had no interest in getting baptised.'

My owners may love Scilly, but I'm no silly dog.

An Eve Under the Family Tree

V.E. DAY – what could it mean? Very exciting, perhaps? Certainly, everyone seemed to be very energetic. We had plenty of callers at the Vicarage. Each visitor had to be given a welcoming bark. The Vicar's wife had stuck some Union Jacks in the flower containers near the front door.

At Church, it was very entertaining. On the Saturday before, a small group of people came to put together an exhibition of drawings, poems and accounts of the Second World War. These had mostly come from the children but some people had sent in things they had kept, such as ration books, gas masks and newspaper cuttings.

I went over to encourage them when the Vicar's wife took them some tea and some cakes iced with V.E. Apart from the odd stroke, no one took much notice of me. They were very engaged in what they were doing.

Monday was a holiday, so the Vicar's wife was at home. In the morning, we went to Trench, near Telford, to see Peggy and John. They always make me welcome, which is more than can be said for their cats. However, I get my own back. In the course of exploring, I usually find the cats' food and have a good taste – very enjoyable!

Back at St. Mark's there was more activity. The bells rang out. Red, white and blue streamers were entwined round the chancel screen. Union Jacks hung from the pulpit. People were going round the exhibition. I felt rather out of it.

As if sensing this, the Vicar lifted me up to look at a page from the

Daily Mirror for V.E. Day 1945.

'Look!' he said. There's one of your ancestors.'

Sure enough, there was a drawing of a dachshund, not wearing a smart fur coat like mine, but still a dachshund, leaping up. It was pleasing to see how many people went to look at my ancestor, though I am not sure what the girl standing next to him was supposed to be doing. She was called Jane, and she had lost most of her clothes. Very extraordinary.

St. Enodoc's and the Golfers

'Fore!'

I stood still and looked in the direction from where the shout had come. There was a man wearing bright coloured check trousers and a peaked cap; he was waving a stick around in an agitated manner. I gave him a hard stare, wondering what he expected me to do about it.

The Vicar's wife came up to me and gave him an even harder stare.

'We are on a public footpath. Kindly let us pass,' she said.

'But you are on the fairway, right in front of the green,' the man shouted back.

'The notice distinctly said we were to follow the white stones,' she replied. 'And these are... Oh dear, they are not white stones but white boards.' She clipped my lead to my collar and led me away, and we went looking for the white stones that marked the path across the golf course. The man in the checked trousers hit the ball and a piece of turf flew into the air. The ball remained where it was.

'It's a selfish game, anyway,' she said. 'Why do they have to take up so much room?'

We were walking across the golf course because we had just left the Vicar at the little Church of St. Enodoc that is in the middle of the course. He was taking the Sunday afternoon service. Much to his surprise, the Church was full, providing healthy competition with the numbers on the golf course. As the Vicar said, 'We all praise God in our own way.' Somehow, I don't think the man who hit the turf instead of the ball, was uttering words of praise.

For many years, until about the time that St. Mark's was built, St.

Enodoc's Church was almost completely buried in the sand. Once a year there was a service, when the Vicar was lowered on a rope into the church through the roof. While the church was being built in Pensnett, this little church was being dug out of the sands.

I didn't know all this, of course, but I heard the Vicar telling his wife all about it, when we got back to the Vicarage at St. Minver's in Cornwall, where we were staying. We were doing holiday duty, which meant the Vicar had to take services at three churches on Sundays and we all relaxed the rest of the time. Perhaps relaxed is not the right word, since the Vicar and his wife were always taking me on long walks across stretches of sand, through harvested corn fields (very prickly on your pads) and along miles of country footpaths, which usually ended in more stretches of sand.

Still, it all made a change. Instead of getting on a bus at High Oak, it was across to Padstow by ferry. Dodging golf balls came as a relief to dodging traffic on Pensnett High Street. However, golfers and car-drivers have one thing in common. They always think it's their right of way.

The Max Factor

'JESUS SAID, 'You did not choose me. I chose you,' said the Vicar out aloud, as he tapped the words into his word processor. I looked up from the armchair, where I was taking my after lunch nap. Pieces off the Sunday roast had been particularly pleasing and my world seemed complete.

The Vicar went on, 'Some people say that our family is given to us but we choose our friends.' It did not occur to me then that the theory was soon to be tried out.

The Vicar's wife came in.

'We must be going to collect Jubilee's friend,' she said. 'I do hope they will get on.'

My lead was attached to my collar. The Vicar left his word-processing and all three of us set off for Tennyson Street to collect 'my friend'.

When we arrived, the family came to meet us.

'I'll just get Max,' said the man, who went inside the house and immediately returned with a glossy, black, smooth-haired dachshund.

'Here's your little friend!' said the Vicar's wife brightly.

'That's as maybe,' I thought, standing my ground as we eyed one another up. Max, apparently, has a long pedigree, and a nose to go with it. With the latter, he moved towards me and began sniffing all over me. Friendship is one thing, but familiarity something else. I growled at him and glared as hard as I could.

'I'm sure they'll get on, in time,' said the Vicar's wife, attaching a lead to Max's collar.

'Yes,' said the Vicar, 'and we could name them "Clarke" and "Redwood"!'

What this meant, I had no idea, but there was little time for further speculation as I felt a tug at my lead. We were off back to the Vicarage, with the Vicar leading me, and his wife bringing up the rear with a somewhat reluctant Max. Like Lot's wife, he kept looking back, longing for Tennyson Street.

Usually, I enjoy some free time in the Coppice but, because of my friend Max, I was kept on my lead all the way. When we reached home, we went into the garden so that Max could get used to it. We went up onto the lawn to play ball but Max refused to play. Instead, he limited himself to one corner, dug himself under a particularly prickly bush and refused to come out. A throaty growl was his only response to the invitations offered by the Vicar and his wife. All this went on for some time.

'Well, he can't stay there,' said the Vicar.

'He certainly can't,' said his wife. 'We are supposed to be taking him out to tea with us.'

I did my best to help by giving him a good 'barking to' but he simply dug down deeper. Unceremoniously, I was removed from the scene while the Vicar's wife resorted to bribery. The promise of food worked a treat. Max decided to come out and he was once more back on the lead.

The house where we went for tea was warm and welcoming. There were rabbits, guinea pigs and pigeons as well as two other dogs to greet us. Max almost let the side down by trying to get in the box where a guinea pig was convalescing, but I have to admit that, on the whole, he did not disgrace the honour of the dachshunds. When it was time for us to leave, he was quite at home. Indeed, there he has been ever since. The family had always wanted a dachshund – and I wasn't available…

From time to time, I have seen Max in the Coppice. He is well settled with his new family. Do I miss my friend? Well, as you humans say, 'It's nice when they come and nice when they go'.

Dog in a Manger

'*A COLD COMING we had of it, just the worst time of the year
For a journey, and such a long journey.*'

The Vicar was in one of his poetic moods and exaggerating again.

The car was warm and comfortable, but there were three of them: the Vicar, his wife and John, their younger son. They didn't have a camel between them but they did have me curled up on the back seat, snuggling against the Vicar's wife. I am not sure how wise they are, but you could definitely say we were from the East, as we made our way across the hills into Wales. There were gifts too. I saw the Vicar put them in the back of the car before we set out. We were on our way to see the vicar's daughter, Mary, her husband, Andrew, and their new baby. Mary and Andrew were both vicars and shared nine parishes around Aberystwyth. Now, they had an additional responsibility, a new baby.

After a drive which lasted nearly two and a half hours and which took us up into the mountains that lie behind Aberystwyth, we arrived at the Vicarage, or Y Ficerdy, as they call it in Welsh, at Ponterwyd. On the other side of the road, there was a shepherd, on what looked like a small tractor, looking after the sheep. Jess, the result of a relationship between one of my distant relatives and a sheep dog, came bounding out of the Vicarage. She is so full of energy and today was no exception. She ran round excitedly, as the Vicar took the presents out of the car. We went into the house, where we found Mary and Andrew with the baby, who was lying, swaddled in a blanket, in a carrying chair.

There was a hush. Nobody said anything. They just looked at the baby in wonder.

'Why's she called Joanna?' asked John, breaking the silence.

'Because Joanna was one of the women who witnessed the Resurrection,' said Mary.

'New birth and Resurrection,' the Vicar murmured almost to himself. I edged forward to get a closer look. She was so tiny. I sniffed the blanket.

'We can't have that!' A pair of hands reached down and picked me up. I don't know what all the fuss is about. They were looking and I was sniffing. Could it be a case of a dog in the manger?

I was carried out into the garden. Jess followed. Soon, she was running round, picking up sticks, while I, at a more sedate pace, explored each shrub in turn. On the hillside opposite, the sheep of Ysbyty Cynfyn continued to graze. Inside the house, I suppose, the humans continued to gaze at the baby.

Christmas, it seemed, had come early to Wales.

Hello, Kim. Do you Bark German?

A s Christmas draws near, there are plenty of visitors to the Vicarage but they mainly come to see the Vicar and his wife, though some also make a fuss of me.

The Confirmation Class brings some of the children from the top end of the Sunday School and we have great fun, or rather had great fun, until the Vicar insisted I was banished from the room, as I was becoming what he called 'a distraction'.

There are many lessons that we can teach you humans, but it would seem that the Vicar hasn't heard of St. Francis.

One Saturday afternoon, a venerable land rover arrived on our drive. Out jumped Adrian, who had come to fix up the lights for the Sunday School play.

'I can see you've brought a visitor to see Jubilee,' said the Vicar.

I bounded out of the Vicarage and looked up into the cab. Could it be another miniature dachshund, or perhaps a Yorkie? No, it was Kim – a German shepherd. We had met before but this was the first time she had been to the Vicarage. She looked down at me with her large enquiring eyes. In fact, as far as I was concerned, everything was large. She seemed uncertain what to do next, so I started to bark.

Adrian soon coaxed her out onto the drive and we ran round each other – though she did most of the running. All four of us set out for a walk to the top of Barrow Hill The light was beginning to fade. The two men seemed deep in conversation, while I explored the undergrowth for new and familiar smells. Kim ran round all over the place and, every so often, seemed to want to round me up, but then, she is a shepherd! It was getting darker and, in the distance, lights shone from the houses and street-lamps. We made our way down the steep side of the hill, to the track that leads to the coppice. By the time we had got back to the Vicarage, Kim and I were getting on quite well. If it wasn't exactly 'the lion lying down with the kid', it was the dachshund reaching an understanding with the German Shepherd.

Our masters were still talking, of course. Much of it seemed to be about lights, though I did hear the Vicar say, 'When it comes to work, it seems to me that you do it, John organizes it and I pray about it.' They both laughed. It would seem that it wasn't only the dogs who enjoyed running circles round each other.

Finally, the land rover rattled off into the darkness, with Kim back on board. The Vicar held his breath as the land rover negotiated the lych-gate. Adrian gave a reassuring toot of triumph, indicating that both wing mirrors had got through unscathed. We returned to the Vicarage; he went off to reflect on his play and what constitutes real work, while I spread myself out in front of the fire. The light still shines in the darkness.

The Human Puppy

HE CAME TOWARDS ME, looking at me, looking me straight in the eye. I had caught glimpses of him, of course, and his name is often to be heard in the Vicarage, but we had never actually met. While I must have seemed strange to him, his eyes were bright and unflinching. Our noses almost touched, as he brushed against me and I felt his warmth.

He gurgled with delight. Like me, he was moving on four legs but, unlike me, he was a human puppy!

He reached out with his front paw, or hand, as humans call it. I turned over on to my back to be tickled, kicking my legs up in the air but, instead, he grabbed a handful of my fur and started to tug.

'Don't do that, Harry,' his mother called. 'Jubilee doesn't like it.'

Actually, I didn't mind at all, since it was not a vicious tug, more an attempt at exploration of my (though I say it myself) handsome coat. The baby scampered away, on all fours, with all the enthusiasm I put into chasing after squirrels, when I can see them. He made straight for the kitchen and was stopped, only just in time, from putting his paws – I mean hands – into my dinner! I looked in amazement. Humans may be late with my dinner sometimes. They may not always provide me with the kind of food I like, but this was the first time that one of them tried to share it with me.

We are now safely home from Milton Keynes, leaving Harry's parents, the vicar's elder son, Andrew, and his wife, to get him ready for his Baptism. I think the Vicar there will find him quite a handful. Let's hope he doesn't try to drink the water in the font!

The Vicar here is beginning to think about Christmas. He looks at me lying on a cushion at just the right angle in front of the fire. I can hear him thinking aloud: 'When God came down at Christmas, he didn't come to stoop down and give us an encouraging pat, or to shout at us from above, or to put down the odd tasty morsel. He came down to our level. He came as a baby, to join in our life and to look us straight in the eye.'

The Vicar starts to sing softly, 'He came down to earth from heaven, who is God and Lord of all, and his shelter was a stable and his cradle was stall; with the poor and mean and lowly, lived on earth our Saviour Holy.' I don't move. There's no need, since you can't, in the animal kingdom, get much closer to the earth than a dachshund.

Asses Milk!

'THERE IS A GREEN HILL far away,' sang the Vicar.

'It might be green far away,' said his wife, 'but ours is covered in snow!'

I have always liked snow but it was a bit unexpected on a Good Friday. Soon they were both well wrapped up in jumpers and waterproofs, and we were off for our morning walk down Vicarage Lane.

Since the snow covered the litter and the broken glass, and it was still quite early, the coppice looked very inviting to one who, like me, enjoys running through the snow, though it can be rather cold underneath. The Vicar's wife wanted to get an extra pint of milk to take to the children's workshop, due to take place later that morning in the church. She always takes a plastic bag on these walks, to pick up the litter. She crossed the road to the shop, leaving me burrowing beneath each lamppost for new smells.

When she returned, we set off up Elgar Crescent towards Barrow Hill. It had a picture-book look about it in the snow, and I looked around to see if there were any sledges. Unusually, there were no children to be seen. We started our climb, when suddenly two ponies came trotting across. They had escaped from the stakes to which they had been attached by traveling folk, and were looking for food. I barked, but it made no difference. One made straight for the Vicar's wife, who tried to push it away.

'Don't just stand there,' she shouted to the Vicar. 'Look, it's trying to bite me. Ow! It has!'

'It must be hungry,' said the Vicar. 'All the grass is covered up.'

'Why don't you do something? I don't want to be a pony's breakfast.'

The Vicar ran towards her. 'Give me the bag. He thinks you've got food in there and not all the rubbish you've picked up.' He grabbed the bag and ran off, with the pony in hot pursuit. The Vicar's wife put me back on my lead. As we turned for home, the Vicar ran after us, without the pony.

'How did you stop him following us?' asked his wife.

'It was quite simple,' he said, sounding quite pleased with himself. 'He only wanted the bag, so I threw it.'

'You threw it?' said the Vicar's wife, in a tone of disbelief and exasperation. 'You've thrown away the milk!'

The Vicar went running back and returned with a ragged plastic bag and a milk-bottle with just a drain left in the bottom.

'Well,' he said, trying to make the best of it, 'there's enough for our coffee.'

I sensed it was going to be one of those days.

We returned to the Vicarage and soon the Good Friday workshop started up in the Church. I was left in charge of the Vicarage, but when the time for the walk up the hill came around, I was let out and joined the party. One of the children, Victor, had brought a sledge. This was very exciting as I was able to run up and down the hill with him. There

were those ponies, now munching some hay that had been brought to them.

As the Vicar said, they looked as if butter wouldn't melt in their mouths, but our milk certainly had!

Easter Thoughts

'BEAR YE one another's burdens.'

The Vicar tapped out the words on his word processor. I looked at him from the armchair in which I was sitting, wondering if he was remembering 'one of the last occasions when he tried to do that.

It was just after Easter. We were in Wales, visiting the Vicar's daughter, Mary, son-in-law, Andrew, granddaughter, Joanna, and Jess, the dog. Walking along the beach near Newquay, we were on a long circular walk that would bring us back to the car we had left parked in the grounds of a country club. As usual, Jess insisted on being thrown pieces of drift-wood to chase after, while I preferred to dig and scratch in the sand and sniff under the rocks and shingle for smells not readily available to us Midland hounds.

Suddenly, we came across a stream of water that poured over the shingle and joined the sea. If we wanted to continue our walk, we had to get across. We walked up and down, looking for the shortest and the shallowest way to cross. There were no helpful stepping-stones.

'We shall have to paddle,' said son-in-law Andrew, removing his socks and shoes.

'But we're wearing tights!' wailed the women.

'And what about the dog?' I wondered. Jess was already following Andrew across the stream, but I had no intention of plunging in and getting my tummy wet.

'Look!' said Andrew. 'It's not very deep.'

The rest looked doubtful and then Andrew added, 'I'll come back and carry you, and Charles can bring Jubilee.'

While Andrew carried, Mary first and then Daphne across the stream, the Vicar removed his socks and shoes and rolled up his trouser legs. With his jacket over one arm and with me in the other, he gingerly put one foot in the water. Immediately, he gave a yell and pulled it out again. 'It's freezing!'

By now, the others were all safely over the stream. Jess was sitting there, looking rather smug, I thought, as the Vicar tried again. Tucked under his right arm, I felt very unsafe, as the Vicar swayed above me and the waters swirled beneath.

'This is terrible!' he cried, lifting first one foot and then the other. 'Now my trouser-legs have started to unroll. They'll get soaked. I'll have to put you down, Jubilee. We're half-way over now. You can swim the rest.'

I couldn't!

'Pick him up!' shouted the Vicar's wife. 'It's far too cold for Jubilee.'

With his teeth chattering, the Vicar reached down to pick me up again, and succeeded in soaking the cuff and lower part of his shirt-sleeve, while the water that rolled off me trickled down his waist. The others shouted encouraging words and told him to think of St. Christopher. With a wet shirt, damp trousers and feet that he claimed were turning blue, the Vicar arrived on the other side. Without much ceremony, he put me down.

'Poor Jubilee!' said his wife solicitously, rubbing me with her handkerchief. The Vicar's teeth were still chattering, but I thought I heard him say that St. Christopher hadn't been expected to carry a soggy doggy.

Yes, I was very interested to hear what the Vicar was going to write about carrying one another's burdens!

Kicking Against the Prickles

'THIS IS AN EASY WALK of some five and a half miles. For little effort, the walker is rewarded with great views'.

The vicar's daughter closed the guidebook and we started off on this 'easy' walk. There were seven of us: the Vicar and his wife, the Vicar's daughter, Mary (also a vicar), her husband Andrew (yet another vicar), their daughter Joanna (who will tell you that she's nearly three, though her birthday comes at the end of October), Jess the dog and myself. With three vicars in the party, I thought, it's bound to be a very holy walk and I'm very much into holes – being bred that way.

We set off up a wooded footpath, which joined a forestry track. Jess, as I have said before, likes to chase after sticks, which she expects people to throw. This means that she usually walks, or runs, about five times as far as the rest of us. I have no interest in fetching sticks, or anything else, and it was beginning to get very warm. Joanna was now being carried on her dad's shoulders. I looked up at Vicar Charles.

'All right,' he said. 'I get the message.' He bent down and carried me. Well, we had been walking for nearly an hour, up hill all the way.

'And on his shoulder, gently laid, and home rejoicing, brought me,' he started to sing.

We climbed over a style. We were now out in the open on some meadowland and still climbing! He put me down again. The shorter grass suits my pads and I even found the energy to roll over and over, carefully avoiding the cowpats – or most of them. The Vicar always makes such a fuss about this sort of thing, usually leaving it to his wife to remove any signs of contact. This time, there was no need, for we soon reached a little stream tumbling down from the hillside. I gratefully lapped the water while some was poured over me, just in case I had become too friendly with any cows.

'From here, we can see spectacular views of Cader Idris and, below us, the River Mawddach joins the estuary winding its way to Barmouth,' Vicar Mary again read from the book. The humans looked suitably impressed but Jess was too busy chasing sticks and I sat panting on the grass.

We came to some rougher pastureland. It was bumpier and there were clumps of scrubby bushes in between. The younger Vicars, Joanna and Jess had soon crossed it, climbed over the ladder-style against the wall, and were sitting on a rock, calling words of encouragement to the rest of us. Soon, the Vicar and his wife were shouting at me from the top of the wall.

'Come along, Jubilee. It's not that difficult.'

However, while I appeared to be sitting in the middle of the field, I was, in fact, being held firmly and painfully underneath. Each time I went to move, the fur underneath tugged relentlessly at my skin.

The Vicar came back for me. 'I suppose you want me to do my "Good Shepherd" act again and carry you,' he said, with an air of exasperation. He tried to pick me up but found that I was indeed trapped, my tummy and my extremities held firmly by a sprawling thistle. Instantly his tone of voice changed as he gently tried to extricate me. At last, I was free, and to show that I was not malingering, made my way to the style unaided.

'Jubilee has proved conclusively what St. Paul discovered,' said the Vicar. 'It's hard to kick against the prickles!' The remark was lost on the others, who were having a drink. We joined them on the rock for a short rest. The estuary was below us and we found ourselves looking down on a helicopter preparing to land, perhaps at Barmouth. The next part of the walk was down hill.

'Jubilee, you've given me another idea for a sermon,' said the Vicar. 'From what we could see outwardly, you looked perfectly all right. How often we fail to notice what's going on inside a person – something Jesus never did.'

I thought it would have been more to the point if they had seen what was going on underneath, never mind the inside. Leaving him to talk to himself, I set off down the hill to join the others. I sensed that we had still got some way to go on this walk… and I wasn't wrong.

Carys Mair Arrives

'I'LL TAKE JUBILEE with me,' said the Vicar's wife.

'Take me where?' I wondered. It was obvious that she meant it, as my bedding had been rolled up, and a bowl of mince covered in cling-film was all ready to go. The doorbell rang and there was Barbara. She is the owner of Morgan, a recent houseguest who had given us all a lively time.

'Now, are you sure you're going to be all right?' the Vicar's wife asked as she carried me to Barbara's car, where Morgan was waiting.

'Well, that all depends,' I thought, only she wasn't talking to me, but to the Vicar.

'I'm sure I can manage for one night,' he said. 'Remember me to them all in Wales.' By all, he meant Vicar Andrew, Vicar Mary, Joanna, who will be three at the end of this month, and Jess the dog. I little knew then, and neither did any of them, that by the same time the following day, the new addition to the family in Wales would be five hours old!

Our journey down was uneventful but, later that evening, Barbara said it was like the Keystone cops. Morgan and I were bundled about in the car as we rushed backwards and forwards down narrow, mountainous, country lanes, just missing Andrew and Mary in their car as they sped off to hospital in Aberystwyth. Apparently, it was all because the waters had broken. I was puzzled about this, as the last time we had problems with water in the Vicarage, the Vicar simply called a plumber.

After this, Morgan and I scarcely got a look in, though there was plenty going on – what was later described as a display of Celtic fireworks. I never actually saw any fireworks myself, but I was probably asleep in my basket at the time.

Carys Mair! That's the name of the new arrival. We have yet to meet as, when we left Wales, Mother and baby were still in hospital. Joanna is very proud of her little sister and, judging by the busy confident way she bustles around, I am sure she will be a great help to her mummy and daddy in looking after her. However. I will admit to being just a little apprehensive when Joanna, by way of a rehearsal, tried to pick me up by my back leg.

I have heard them say that the baby looks like her daddy, with a shock of dark hair, but as the name means 'Beloved of Mary', they are off to a promising start.

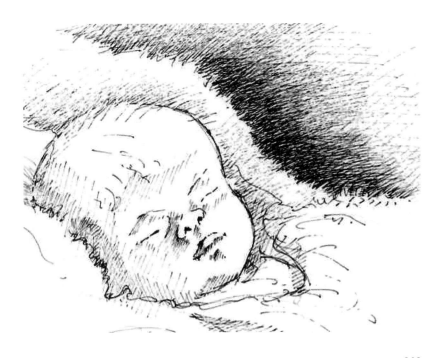

A Good Amen

'HAVEN'T YOU FINISHED your contribution to the Parish Magazine yet?' the Vicar's wife asked, as the train bringing us back from Aberystwyth made its way between the frost-covered fields and snow-capped mountains. 'I think it should be your New Year's resolution, not to say Millennium resolution, to get your writing in on time.'

The Vicar looked across the rattling carriage, to where his wife was sitting, and our eyes met. Stretched out on a seat next to her, curled up in her furry hat and feeling the benefit of the nearby heater, I yawned and, since it was his problem and not mine, I closed my eyes again.

It had been a busy day. Up at the crack of a cold dawn, dragged down Vicarage Lane, trying to avoid black-ice patches, I had gratefully scrambled into the car, which I thought was to take us to Wolverhampton. I wondered what was up. It turned out that we were going to Aberystwyth, to see the Vicar's daughter and granddaughters.

On our arrival, we walked through the little town thronged with Christmas shoppers and then on to the beach, which was deserted. The sea was calm. The waves lapped the sand, as if to say, 'We've seen so many Christmases.' I was able to have a free run and to explore just where I wanted.

At last, we met up with Vicar Mary, Joanna and Carys. Carys is still a very young pup, whose needs are simple: feeding and changing. She looks at me, as I look at her, in wonder. In contrast, three-year-old Joanna calls my name, 'Jubilee!' She is already making up her mind about the world and her place in it. After all, she has just been an Angel in her nursery school nativity. Sitting at the table, crayoning, I hear her call out, 'Say Amen!' She is clearly echoing her mother. Confirming this impression, she adds, 'And we shall now sing Jesus Price.'

The Vicar is still chuckling to himself about this on the train home.

'Well,' he explained, 'Jesus did, indeed, come for the Prices, and there must be many in Wales, but he also came for the Joneses, the Smiths and, in fact, for all the families on earth.'

I fall into a deeper sleep. After all, it is given to you humans to try to make sense of the world and to do something about it. For us dogs, we simply accept it as it is and take everything as it comes. So many of us depend on you, so we hope you get it right and, as Joanna says, 'Let's have a good Amen.'

Better a Tail-wagger
than a Tongue-wagger

IN HIS STUDY, the Vicar has one of those tear-off calendars with a witty, or wise, saying for each day of the week.

'Preach, not because you have to say something, but because you have something to say,' he read aloud, while working on his letter for this magazine.

I looked up at him from my new basket. It's made entirely of material with a lovely quilted rim. When it first arrived, I kept capsizing, ending up underneath the basket instead of inside it. The secret, I've discovered, is to get your balance right, by distributing your weight across the basket instead of simply leaning up against one side. As this is a present for me for our new home in Wales, I knew I must learn to master it. I am not going to be laughed at by all those Welsh sheepdogs.

From time to time, before we actually moved there, we had been going down to our new home, and I am beginning to find my way around. I know how to get to the seat on the hill above the Parc Natur Penglais nature reserve, and I enjoy running across the beach. All the same, I shall miss all those who call at the Vicarage. Most people make a fuss of me and, given a chance, or the slightest encouragement, I like to get in on all those meetings. If I'm especially lucky, I work my way up on to someone's lap. Denim and corduroy get me particularly excited. Sometimes the Vicar apologises for my behaviour, though I never see the need. Our visitors enjoy my company, which I am sure is much more stimulating than all those meetings. Some people said, when we were out for a walk, that they always read my column before anything else in the Parish magazine. To be honest, I think the Vicar gets a bit jealous of my popularity.

'How is it, Jubilee, that you seem to have so many friends?' His eye again caught mine. Unable to reply, I just looked at him, wrestling away with his article for the Easter edition. It seemed that he'd forgotten the message that had been on his calendar a few days ago:

'The reason a dog has so many friends – is that his tail wags instead of his tongue!'

News from Mid Wales
(Newyddion o Ganolbarth Cymru)

W E'VE BEEN HERE just over a year now and seen the seasons change. The woods behind us serve as a calendar as well as the scene for my daily walks. A few weeks ago, they were full of bluebells and all the more welcome this year because, before that, the paths were closed on account of the foot and mouth. The trees are showing off this year's shade of green. Later on will come the blackberries, the crabapples and the chestnuts. Winter is really my best time. Protected by my long fur coat, the cold is simply exhilarating, as I explore different trees and bushes, watched by all kinds of birds, and the many squirrels scampering up and down the branches. In the winter and early spring, I explore the local beaches, now closed to me for the summer months.

The Vicar (Yes, he still gets called that) and his wife still scamper around the town in all seasons. Daphne can be seen pushing a trolley round Somerfields, another kind round our hospital and yet another, containing the younger granddaughter, Carys, round the ruins of Edward the First's castle, where swings and climbing frames have replaced the engines of siege and ballistae. Perhaps, unknowingly inspired by these ancient conflicts, Carys seeks to keep at bay those who would challenge her right to the driving seat on the toy bus.

Vicar Charles does his own kind of scampering. He takes services at our local church, and he was very thrilled to be asked to celebrate Communion at our Methodist Church. He says that the training he received at Bromley was a great help! As he also takes services outside Aberystwyth, it has been necessary for him to learn Welsh. The granddaughters are learning to speak both languages, so Charles and Daphne have been going to classes. Going back to school, as pupils, has been an interesting experience for them both. Charles says that it's amazing how quickly you recall the old ways. From my basket in the sitting room, I see him wrestling with his homework and once I saw him take a quick look at Daphne's answers, while she was getting my supper ready. When Daphne saw what he was up to, he denied it was cheating.

'Just checking – that's all!'

Their teacher has told them to get as much practice as possible. I was with them when they went into our local fish-shop.

'*Dw i eisiau dau bysgodyn i swper os gwelwch yn dda,*' said Charles.

'Don't speak that language,' the fishmonger replied, with a strong Welsh accent.

It was enough to make a dog laugh or *ci chwerthin*. That's right – I'm a *ci* in Welsh. When I come to think of it, we dogs can be the key, in any language, to promoting good will. We went to Joanna's Primary School, out in the country at Llanafon, for Red Nose Day. The forty children in the school had prepared various games and stalls to raise funds for children in need. Charles, having had some practice over the years, guessed the number of red Smarties in the jar. The prize was the jar of Smarties, and he was conscious of forty pairs of envious eyes fixed on him when he went to receive the prize from the head teacher. All that excitement was quickly forgotten, when the children saw me. Soon, I was surrounded by youngsters, who all wanted to stroke and tickle me. It was absolute bliss.

At our home, I continue to be the chief welcomer. We've been pleased to see many familiar faces from Pensnett, and there is photographic evidence to prove it. We look forward to seeing you and saying, '*Croeso!*'

Ffarwel i bawb. Remember, the dog is the real *ci*!

Final Chapter

'**G**OOD LUCK IN YOUR EXAM!' said Eifion, a young man whom we often meet on our walks through Penglais Woods, with his spaniel, Molly. I looked up from playing with Molly; I had completed my training years ago and won a rosette. What was this about an exam?

It was a relief to know that it was the Vicar and his wife who were to take an exam, and not myself. I had noticed that, on our walks, he would try talking to me in Welsh, but I hadn't understood the full significance of, 'You're probably the only one who understands.'

A few weeks later, we were on our way to Meifod, the site of this year's National Eisteddfod.

'You may not be allowed in, Jubilee,' said the Vicar.

'That's why we are going to carry him in this carrier,' said his wife determinedly.

We arrived at the gate.

'Is it all right to bring him in?' asked the Vicar nervously.

'All right? Of course it's all right!' said one of the stewards expansively. 'Let's have a look at him.'

Prince Charles himself could not have received a warmer welcome. Once inside, we walked round the various tents. The National Assembly tent offered us tea and fruit, with a fresh bowl of water for me.

'We can't turn this down,' said the vicar's wife.

'No, it's the first time we've ever got anything out of them!'

The highlight came in the Learners' tent. Much to my surprise, I heard the Vicar and his wife called to the platform, to receive their certificates. They had passed their exam. Everybody clapped, I barked. Mary, the Vicar's daughter, on whose lap I was sitting, said, 'Sh!' Joanna and Carys laughed, delighted not to be the ones being told off. Nobody really minded. As the vicar and his wife returned to their places, holding their certificates, I thought – rosettes are better but, then, they are only human.

Titles already published

Shapeshifters at Cilgerran – Liz Whittaker £5.95
Germs – Dai Vaughan £5.95
Cunval's Mission – David Hancocks £5.95
When the Kids Grow Up – Ken James £6.95
The Church Warden – Lillian Comer £7.95
The Fizzing Stone – Liz Whittaker £4.95
A Dragon To Agincourt – Malcom Pryce £7.95
Aberdyfi: Past and Present – Hugh M Lewis £6.95
Aberdyfi: The Past Recalled – Hugh M Lewis £6.95
Ar Bwys y Ffald – Gwilym Jenkins £7.95
Black Mountains – David Barnes £6.95
Choose Life! – Phyllis Oostermeijer £5.95
Clare's Dream – J Gillman Gwynne £4.95
Cwpan y Byd a dramâu eraill – J O Evans £4.95
Dragonrise – David Morgan Williams £4.95
Dysgl Bren a Dysgl Arian – R Elwyn Hughes £9.95
In Garni's Wake – John Rees £7.95
Stand Up and Sing – Beatrice Smith £4.95
The Dragon Wakes – Jim Wingate £6.95
The Wonders of Dan yr Ogof – Sarah Symons £6.95
You Don't Speak Welsh – Sandi Thomas £5.95

For more information about this innovative imprint,
contact Lefi Gruffudd at lefi@ylolfa.com
or go to www.ylolfa.com/dinas.
A Dinas catalogue is also available.